Addison Steele is a pseudo
book editor.

Addison Steele

Upward Nobility

How to Win the Rat Race
without Becoming a Rat

Futura Publications Limited

A Futura Book

First published in Great Britain by
Futura Publications Limited in 1979

Copyright © 1978 by Addison Steele

Grateful acknowledgement is made to Alfred A.
Knopf, Inc., for permission to quote from
Something Happened by Joseph Heller, copyright
© 1974 by Joseph Heller.

ISBN 0 7088 1690 8

Printed in Great Britain by
Hazell Watson & Viney Ltd
Aylesbury, Bucks

Futura Publications Limited
110 Warner Road
Camberwell, London SE5

For three "perfect bosses"—
they know who they are because I told them

"A man should always consider how much he has more than he wants, and how much more unhappy he might be than he really is."

Joseph Addison and Sir Richard Steele
The Spectator, no. 574 (July 30, 1714)

Contents

Introduction

THE idea for this book first came to me when I was having lunch with Carol, a talented, ebullient, and extremely likable editor in a large publishing house. On this occasion, however, Carol's usual ebullience was not in evidence, and, midway through the second martini, she told me why.

"Victor Scott's leaving, as I'm sure you've heard. They're giving the managing editorship to Steve Turner." She took another sip. "Steve's been in the company only two years, and I've been there six. I've brought in three books that went for over a hundred thousand dollars in paperback and you tell me what *he's* brought in."

I waited for the usual complaint. "Sexism?" I asked.

She paused and gave the matter some thought. "No," she said, "I really don't think so. It wouldn't matter if Steve were a woman. The main reason for his success is that he's so damn political. He's a self-promoter. He's so busy cultivating his corporate image and buttering up the top people that I frankly don't think he has any *time* left to devote to his list."

She looked at me plaintively. "I know it must sound like sour grapes. But for God's sake, you *know* what I've brought in over there."

I did know. Everyone in the industry knew that Carol was a top acquiring editor with an almost uncanny commercial sense, and that moreover she was one of the few book editors in New York who still knew how to use a pencil. She was also regarded as completely straight; and I had heard it said, more than once, that it was remarkable how little sense she had of her own power. I knew from my own twelve years in the industry that these were not exactly the qualities likely to propel her to the top of the organization.

So did she.

"It isn't as though nobody ever told me you have to be political," she said. "Just look at the how-to-succeed books that have come out in the last few years. I'll tell you something: they were right all along. Thinking their advice amoral, I went along on my merry little way, and screwed up my whole career."

"Are you so sure of that?" I asked.

"What do you mean?"

I looked her right in the face and asked her the $30,000 question. (That's what the managing editor's job would have been worth, at most.)

"Did you really want success that badly? *Were you willing to pay the price to get it?*"

She smiled ruefully. "No," she replied, "I suppose not."

And we looked at each other with the understanding born of shared values and similar aspirations. For even as I asked Carol that crucial question, I already suspected what her answer would be.

And suddenly an idea, which had been germinating for years somewhere in my subconscious, sprang to the fore.

"Carol," I said excitedly, "I'm going to write a book!"

"All editors want to write a book," was her—I thought ungenerous—response. "It's an occupational hazard."

"It's going to be about people like us," I continued, "people who won't—or can't—play corporate games. And why they shouldn't have to. And why they wouldn't be happy if they did."

Always commercial-minded, even under stress, Carol retorted:

"Oh, great! A book about how to fail in the corporate jungle. *That* should sell about seventy copies!"

But I had my answer ready.

"No. In its own peculiar way, this is going to be a book about success. *Personal* success, not corporate success.

"Surely you of all people know they're not the same thing."

Interest and skepticism vied for a position on her face.

"Sure, *I* feel that way. And *you* feel that way. But how many other people feel that way?"

"Thousands, I bet." I took a hefty swallow of my own second martini. (Well, publishing lunches are known for that, in case you haven't heard.) "Maybe," I went on, sales figures glistening behind my eyeballs, "maybe even . . . millions."

SITTING here behind my typewriter now, the effects of the martinis having long since been dissipated, I have no cause to change my opinion. I do believe that there are many thousands of working men and women—talented, bright, well-educated, and productive—who are simply not fitted by temperament or inclination to mold themselves into corporate mannikins or spend their working and nonworking hours polishing their executive images and planning survival strategy. These are people who have learned through their own experiences that the game simply isn't worth the candle. But many of them feel exceedingly guilty. The game is *said* to be worth the candle. One is *supposed* to want to climb the ladder at any price. Giving up friendships within the company, being concerned with image instead of substance, weighing the ramifications of every single word uttered in a working day, in a working week, in a working year—these are *not* sacrifices too great to be tolerated. Books say so. Friends say so. Co-workers say so.

And so, when these people choose not to play the game, they feel there is something wrong with them.

Or, conversely, when they are browbeaten into playing the game, they play it badly. And then they wonder why it doesn't work for them when it works for so many others.

Well, if you are one of those people, this book is for you. And the thesis of it is this:

1. *There is nothing wrong with you. There is* everything *wrong with the game.*

2. *It is the corporation's game, created to suit their interests, not your interests, nor the interests of any other employee.*

3. *If you played the game, and if you "won" the game, it would not make you happy.*

UPWARD NOBILITY

I

Are You *"Upwardly Noble"?*

I am assuming that you are an ordinary garden-variety nice person. Not necessarily a saint who has offered your blood to the blood bank or your eyes to the eye bank or your body to science. Perhaps you have never helped a little old lady across the street or given huge sums of money to the indigent or volunteered to empty bedpans in a hospital ward. Perhaps you sometimes have even undertipped a waiter, yelled at your spouse, if you have one, or neglected to water your plants over a long holiday weekend. But I am assuming this much: that you do *not* want to spend your life locking horns with other people, pretending to friendships you do not feel or, conversely, abandoning friends you like but who are of no "value" to you in your career. I am also assuming that you are more concerned with what you accomplish than how you appear to others; that you would rather be yourself than put on a corporate mask, and that, indeed, dissembling of any kind depresses and exhausts you.

Just an ordinary, garden-variety, run-of-the-mill nice person, to whom all the wisdom of the modern age says:

"Friend, it won't work!"

Well, maybe by other people's lights it *won't* work. But by your lights it *does* work and it *has* worked. Because you are living your life as you want to live it when so many people are not. Because you have not allowed yourself to make the endless number of compromises that the blindly ambitious make every day of their lives as a matter of course. Because you have lived your life fully in the present, while the more political in your organization have sacrificed every hour of every day to a "future" which, at best, is precarious, at worst, illusory.

And if *their* dreams go unrealized, as a great many will, these people are likely to be far more bitter than you. Because they have given up their day-to-day happiness, their individualism, and occasionally, even, their very souls.

That sounds pretty melodramatic. And yet I have interviewed countless numbers of people who put the dilemma in just those terms. None of them were smug or self-righteous. None of them pretended to know what would work for other people. No one I spoke to thought he had cornered the market on morality. But each expressed an unease about his own life and how he wanted to live it. Some were rethinking their own ambitions in the light of the compromises they had made and the negligible rewards they had to show for it. Some, who had risen to a managerial level, were wondering if they hadn't been happier earlier in their careers. And some, who had adamantly refused—like Carol—even to consider remolding their personalities to fit the corporate stereotype, were surprisingly philosophical about being left behind on the middle rung of the ladder.

The people I spoke to, with one or two exceptions, were all in the publishing industry. I decided to confine myself to publishing for two reasons: First, it is the field in which I have spent my working life, and I was fairly sure I could find a wide sampling of friends and acquaintances who would talk candidly with me. Second, and of more importance to the reader, publishing has long cherished the reputation of being a "gentleman's industry" (no sexist slights intended). Most people I have known over the years originally went into publishing believing it to be different from other businesses—cleaner, nobler, less competitive, more humane. The people who were attracted to publishing, one might therefore conclude, did not see themselves as hard-nosed aggressive types. And, I think, a majority of publishing people agree that publishing is a nice business compared with most others.

But corporations, even the most enlightened, have their own

inherent pressures and irrationalities. The incidents we are going to chronicle here, outrageous as some of them may seem, will come as a shock only to someone who has never worked in a corporation. For the rest, there will be a different shock—the shock of recognition. This is because, to turn Tolstoy's famous dictum around, "all unhappy corporations are unhappy in the same way."

But there are ways in which you can remain happy within the organization and make it serve your particular needs.

Begin by examining your own values. You should go about this as unemotionally as a nineteenth-century Benthamite, weighing the *cost* of certain behavior against the potential *gain* of certain behavior. And if the cost outweighs the gain, then surely it will not be difficult to find the courage to say, "No. It isn't worth it."

Have you seriously considered the cost of getting ahead? The cost to your health? To your peace of mind? To your private life?

Have you weighed the potential gains of such a sacrifice? Will the corporate advancement make you rich? Will it make you happy? Can such advancement be *guaranteed* to take place? Are there circumstances you can't control no matter how you comport yourself? Will the next rung be fulfilling or will it merely be a stepping-stone to the one after that? Is there an end to the treadmill?

A few years ago, at a publishing party, I met the author of one of the better-known how-to-get-ahead-in-business manifestos. I found him in his "power corner"—he was following his own advice of grabbing a corner of the room at any party and letting people come to him—and I buttonholed him about what I considered to be one of the more outrageous lines in his book: "Work without ambition is drudgery."

"Come on!" I said. "Taken to its logical conclusion, that would mean a permanent state of discontent in any job, no matter how prestigious, no matter how glamorous. If you are always angling for the next rung on the ladder, how can you possibly ever enjoy the rung you are on?"

Looking bored by my question, possibly not even understanding it, since obviously he did not think in such terms, the author replied shortly, "If you don't go forward, you go backward." He then turned his attention to some powerful publishing people, of which there was a fair amount. There was no arguing with success—they had all gravitated to his corner.

But I still believe what I said to him that night. How refreshing it would be if people could just take pleasure—keen, immediate pleasure—in the work they are presently involved with, instead of always being concerned with climbing, climbing, climbing. Climbing is so hard on the nervous system. I have known personally too many young, driving executives—mostly men in their late thirties and early forties—who have had crippling and sometimes fatal heart attacks. I have had lunches with too many colleagues who were nursing an ulcer or a spastic colon. And I have seen too much needless fear, as evidenced by hands trembling in a meeting, backs that suddenly go into spasm at the sight of a closed door, and voices that either slide into the upper register or disappear completely when the boss leaves a note on the desk saying, "Please stop by my office right away."

Anyway, let's get back to you and whether you're the sort of person who should—or shouldn't—claw your way to the top.

Probably you already know. But just for fun, why not try your hand at this quiz? It's not especially subtle and there are no "trick" questions, but if you answer it as honestly as you can, it should give you a pretty good indication of your own temperament and needs.

QUIZ NUMBER ONE

1. Day-to-day happiness is extremely important to me.
   a) Agree strongly
   b) Agree moderately
   c) Disagree moderately
   d) Disagree strongly

2. I can dissemble pretty well when I have to.
   a) Agree strongly
   b) Agree moderately
   c) Disagree moderately
   d) Disagree strongly

3. I am envious of friends who are more successful than I am.
   a) Agree strongly
   b) Agree moderately
   c) Disagree moderately
   d) Disagree strongly

4. I am terribly concerned about what other people think of me.
   a) Agree strongly
   b) Agree moderately
   c) Disagree moderately
   d) Disagree strongly

5. I think it's a good idea always to "look busy" at the office.
   a) Agree strongly
   b) Agree moderately
   c) Disagree moderately
   d) Disagree strongly

6. I would not be overjoyed to give up a windowless office that was cool and comfortable for a hot, uncomfortable corner office with a window.
   a) Agree strongly
   b) Agree moderately
   c) Disagree moderately
   d) Disagree strongly

7. It is much simpler to answer one's own phone rather than letting a secretary do it.
   a) Agree strongly
   b) Agree moderately
   c) Disagree moderately
   d) Disagree strongly

8. I have an expensive lifestyle, and I don't want to give it up.
   a) Agree strongly
   b) Agree moderately
   c) Disagree moderately
   d) Disagree strongly

9. I am leery of making sacrifices for anything unless I can be assured of positive results.
   a) Agree strongly
   b) Agree moderately
   c) Disagree moderately
   d) Disagree strongly

10. Leisure activities bore me; I would much rather be at the office.
    a) Agree strongly
    b) Agree moderately
    c) Disagree moderately
    d) Disagree strongly

Scoring

Award yourself the following number of points for each answer:

Question 1: a–0; b–1; c–2; d–3
Question 2: a–3; b–2; c–1; d–0
Question 3: a–3; b–2; c–1; d–0
Question 4: a–3; b–2; c–1; d–0
Question 5: a–3; b–2; c–1; d–0
Question 6: a–0; b–1; c–2; d–3
Question 7: a–0; b–1; c–2; d–3
Question 8: a–3; b–2; c–1; d–0
Question 9: a–0; b–1; c–2; d–3
Question 10: a–3; b–2; c–1; d–0

Evaluation

Score 0–10 points: If you tried to climb too high on the corporate ladder you would be likely to fall off and break both your legs. Very probably, you already know this about yourself. You are too straightforward, too uncalculating, and too much your own person to want to make the necessary compromises to get ahead. Your main ambition is to be happy and fulfilled. You have interests outside your work. You are, according to Michael Maccoby's breakdown of organizational types, a "craftsman," not a "gamesman" or "jungle fighter." This book is aimed right between your eyebrows.

Score 11–20 points: You have a certain amount of healthy ambition, but it is not overwhelming, and there are certain sacrifices you are not prepared to make to bring about your goals. You are at a disadvantage when you try to compete with the more political people in your company. You can't lie as well as they can, you are careless about your corporate image, and, in the middle of a boring meeting, you sometimes find your mind drifting to thoughts of mountain-climbing in the Himalayas or the tennis match you won against the club champion. If *you* try to climb too high on the corporate ladder, you may not notice when one of your co-workers starts sawing away at the very rung upon which you are perched.

Score 20–30 points: You don't need or want this book. Quite probably you didn't buy it. You are a corporate in-fighter and very good at it. Such activity fits your temperament and psychology. It is *you* everyone else has to watch out for. Whatever rung you are on now, you are going higher. Recommended reading for you are Michael Korda's *Power* and *Success,* Michael Maccoby's *The Gamesman,* and Robert J. Ringer's *Winning Through Intimidation.* Quite probably, you have already read them.

II

It's the Company's Chessboard, Old Mate

ANY business organization, by definition, if not always in actual practice, is nonhumanistic and amoral. Granted the existence of many thousands of companies which have—and deserve—the reputation of being exceedingly nice places to work, the fact remains that businesses do not exist to make their employees happy. They do not exist to provide them with stimulating lives or recognition from their peers. Rather, they exist to make money. Almost always, that is their sole purpose. Even when we are discussing a business which makes things of value to society—books, musical instruments, iron lungs, or hearing aids—the *raison d'être* of that organization is not the social good, but profit. This is not to attack the capitalist system: some awfully good things have come about because of the profit motive. But what I'm saying is that the company's interest is in direct conflict with yours:

They want to get the most work out of you for the lowest salary.

But how can they motivate you to work harder without paying you more money?

They offer you nonmonetary "rewards." Rewards that don't cost them much and sometimes don't cost them anything. Rewards that it might never occur to you you wanted, if they didn't tell you you *should* want them. Rewards that will be given to somebody else if you should be so foolish as to turn them down.

Like what, you ask?

Like a wood desk instead of a plastic one. Like a blue carpet if everyone else has gray. Like the opportunity to eat in the executive dining room. Like a company credit card instead of your own personal one.

All things which are of absolutely no use to you whatsoever, either monetarily or by way of greater comfort, a more secure future, or anything else that's really important. These incentives to greater and greater striving provide one thing only:

Status, in the eyes of others.

Now, to be sure, there are *some* rewards worth having. A private office is more pleasant than a cubicle. An office with a door is more comfortable than an office without one. An office with a window is usually—but not always—more desirable than one without. But the *reasons* ambitious people want these things usually have little to do with their inherent desirability. To them, the wood desk is as important as having a door. It is visible proof to other people of their higher status in the company.

I am reminded of a man who headed a department in the company in which I worked. We had moved to a different building, and he was on another floor, so I hardly ever saw him. But a few months after the move, I ran into him on the elevator, and asked him how he was enjoying life in the new building.

He had, he said, a nice window office facing west with an incomparable view of the Hudson River from the forty-fifth floor. The only problem was that the office was stifling. With no buildings to block out the sun, and with the air-conditioning system not yet having been turned on, the heat in the afternoons was well-nigh unbearable. Sometimes he even felt sick to his stomach.

"Well," I said, knowing that Fred could probably get any office he wanted in the department, "why not move to an office without a window? That's what I have, and it's much, much cooler."

Fred looked at me as though I had told him he should sell his children into slavery.

"Oh, I could hardly do that!" he exclaimed. "My ego is more important than my body." So help me, those were his very words.

As I walked back to my cool, pleasant, comfortable, window-less office, I thought to myself that I just couldn't think that way. My ego, always strong, could take care of itself; my body needed all the help it could get!

To be sick to your stomach every afternoon, five days a week, seemed an inordinately high price to pay for status.

But, as you're no doubt already thinking, it would take a pretty cool customer (no pun intended) to turn down a corner window office when it is such a potent symbol in one's place in the pecking order. Companies, handing out symbols in lieu of fatter paychecks, are confident that people will work, compete, fight, *kill* to obtain such symbols. And they are usually right. The cost to them: practically nothing.

Peter, a copywriter, told me about the Kafkaesque situation in his firm:

"They won't give a window office to anyone below the level of supervisor. That's always been their policy. Of course, the copy-writers are in their offices all day long, while the supervisors are either out of the office seeing advertising people or in meetings in the conference room upstairs.

"Right now, it's ridiculous. They've got four copywriters sit-ting in small, inside offices, and there are exactly four—count them, *four!*—large window offices that are not being used by anyone! Debbie actually got up the nerve to complain to our boss about the illogic of it. She got nowhere. All he said was that those offices would have to remain free in case someone was brought in at a higher level or in case someone was promoted.

"Three of those offices have been empty for more than eight months, and the large one has been empty for *two years!* And meanwhile, many of us here, making money for the company, are in totally inadequate quarters. I will never understand the corporate mentality!"

Surely all of you must know of similar situations in your own office.

Another method companies use to keep people working harder for less money is to make them insecure about their own position and future.

Bernice, who until recently worked as Publicity Director for a large publishing conglomerate, told me of one such incident:

"It happened," she said, "at the least likely moment, which made it that much worse. I was feeling happy, relaxed, well-fed, and secure, having been invited by the President of the company to a special lunch at Lutèce, along with the Editor-in-Chief, the Vice-President and General Manager, the Marketing Director, the Advertising Director, and the Art Director. No expense had been spared; the President had been planning this lunch for two weeks. It began with three different varieties of pâté and ended with a divine Grand Marnier soufflé, with meat, fish, and game courses in between. There were several wines served as well as champagne with dessert.

"Unfortunately, I almost choked over the Grand Marnier soufflé. You see, the President picked just this moment to lean forward over the table and say, out of the blue, 'Well, I wonder if any of us will be here a year from now!'

"There was an abrupt pall in the conversation as all these happy, relaxed, sated people suddenly thought, 'My God! What's he trying to tell us?' And we were hardly worried about *him*: he ran the place with a positively dictatorial hand and obviously wasn't going anywhere.

"Well, it's exactly one year later, and, as you know, I've been fired. So have three of the other people who were at this high-powered, supposedly celebratory lunch. And the two remaining people have told me they are quite sure that the bell will also toll for them in the not-too-distant future. As a matter of fact, I have very little doubt that by the time your book is published they'll both be gone."

A horrible story, but hardly unique, except perhaps for the sybaritic circumstances during which it took place. Here's another—just as bad, and unfortunately just as true.

For the past seven years Chuck has been a staff writer for a prestigious magazine. He's a good friend of mine, and I have always found his enthusiasm for the job, the people he works with, and the people he works for to be unfailing. More than once, he has described the place as "a Garden of Eden." Two years ago, he told me over drinks that he had never in five years seen a single instance of jockeying for position, knifing in the back, or any other unpleasantness in the department.

"You see, there's no *reason* to compete with anyone else," he told me. "We all do our own thing, and my success doesn't threaten anybody else, nor does their success threaten me. We're all pulling together to get this magazine out on time, and to make it the best edition we possibly can. We're all friends— we go out together, we drink together, and the morale is terrifically high."

The last time I saw Chuck, however, he had a far different story to tell.

"I've got to get off this damn magazine," he said. "I can't take the politics and backbiting another minute. The people in the department hardly ever *talk* to each other any more. Everyone wants a bigger piece of the pie and, frankly, there's nobody left I feel I can trust."

I asked him how such a radical change could have come about, and in such a relatively short time.

"They brought in this business-school guy to head the editorial department." The expression on Chuck's face was eloquent testimony to his low opinion of the B-school mentality. "He's not an editorial type. He's pure management through and through. And what these guys are taught at business school, you wouldn't believe!"

I asked him to be more specific.

"He took the senior staff members out for drinks. He got a bit smashed, and he told us all—*he actually said this incredible thing in so many words*—that we were all too damned comfortable and too damned happy, and that comfortable, happy people become apathetic about their work. He said his object was to break down the friendships in the office—'You people shouldn't be drinking together, you should be going after each other's jobs!' Then he said that it was a good business technique to keep people nervous and insecure about their own positions."

I had never seen Chuck, who is not a nervous sort, shake like that. Part of it, of course, was sheer rage.

He went on: "The son-of-a-bitch seemed completely oblivious to the idea that any of us would be remotely upset about his plans for the department. He was having a fine old time telling us about his superior management concepts. *Then* he said, looking at us all conspiratorially, that it might be a little rougher than we were used to, but that, for those of us 'who had the stuff,' as he put it, there would be a terrific opportunity to get ahead.

"As far as I'm concerned, I'm getting out. If I had wanted to work in a battlefield, I would have become a professional soldier!"

Chuck smiled grimly. "Well, maybe the time has come anyway for me to move on. Maybe it will be a good thing for my career." I could see he didn't believe a word of what he was saying.

I was horrified by the story. Horrified that one rotten captain could scuttle such a happy ship. Even more, I was horrified that the staff members had allowed it to happen, that they had gone along with his admonition to try and cut each other's throats.

"I'm sorry, Chuck," I said. "I blame the staff as much as the boss. They didn't *have* to start cutting each other up. They didn't *have* to stop being friendly, or going out for drinks. *Why did they do it?* There are certain corporate games you simply don't want to play!"

Chuck looked drained. "The wrong person at the top can poison a whole department, a whole organization, even. Believe me, I've seen it. You tell John that you're thinking of sending him down to Washington for an interview with the President, and you tell Jane that you're thinking of sending *her* down to Washington for an interview with the President, and then you call Tom into your office and explain that you can't decide whether to send John or Jane down to Washington, so you hope he'll watch them both carefully for the next few weeks to see who is putting out better work, and pretty soon none of them are talking to each other. John and Jane are vying for the same plum, and Tom is feeling he's more important than either of them because he's being asked to judge them.

"That's only one example of the sorts of techniques that have been used." Chuck grimaced. *"They work.* You may think you're the nicest, friendliest person in the world, but I want to tell you that in a situation like that, you start looking out for old Number One. And so does everyone else."

"Well," I said, "there's no use arguing about water over the dam. You're leaving, and, at this point, I think you're well out of there. But I still feel that if the department had pulled together, your boss would have been playing his management games in a vacuum."

But even as I said it I knew I was whistling in the dark. In even the nicest department, there are going to be a few latent sharks, and all they need is a little encouragement from the top. All you can do is refuse to play along and keep reminding yourself what *you* want out of your job, not what you are told you *should* want out of your job. After all, both John and Jane had presumably been very happy with their assignments without ever having been sent to Washington to interview the President. If that particular plum had not been dangled in front of their eyes, neither of them might ever have thought of it! As for Tom, who got pleasure out of feeling superior to them both, well, he and people like him are the subjects of our next chapter.

III

The Kindergarten Mentality

BUSINESSES today are bigger and more complex than ever before. Small family-owned operations get gobbled up by huge conglomerates. Sales and profits per year are in the many millions of dollars. We should expect to find at the top of such sophisticated organizations highly sophisticated people: brilliant, innovative, mature.

Brilliant and innovative? Yes, usually. Mature? I'll let *you* be the judge of that.

Here is one peerless example of corporate thinking, taken from my own beloved company.

We were, when this incident took place, housed on a large, single floor of a Manhattan skyscraper in which about eighty percent of the private offices were without doors. *Why* the offices had been constructed this way was anybody's guess. But the result was a situation in which men and women at levels as high as that of Senior Editor worked without privacy or quiet. Typewriters clattered away outside their offices, secretaries chattered away outside their offices, and there was no escape. These people had jobs that required a high level of concentration for long periods of time—reading manuscripts, editing manuscripts, copy editing manuscripts. The privileged twenty percent with doors were usually at a managerial level. Their work, which consisted of such things as overseeing budgets, bringing in authors, and coordinating publishing schedules, required less intense concentration. And they were out of their offices a great deal of the time, anyway, attending meetings.

Not enough room had been allowed for expansion when the company had leased the floor, and the office was overcrowded. Finding space for anyone at any level was a problem, especially in certain departments.

I heard this story from an editor who had worked briefly in our department and transferred to another. I ran into David in the hall.

"Did you hear?" he asked. "Elaine's been promoted to Assistant Editor." Elaine had been an Editorial Assistant, and it was a big step forward for her. "It seems the only office they had available in our department was Karen O'Connell's old office"— Karen had been Assistant Managing Editor, and had resigned to take a Managing Editor's job elsewhere—"and they've moved Elaine in there."

"That's nice," I said.

"Yes. Well, you're not going to believe what Office Services did at nine o'clock this morning!"

"What?" I asked.

"They came and took her door away."

"They *what*???"

David grinned. "They removed the door to Karen's old office. They said that Elaine was not nearly important enough to have a door, and that the only reason they'd moved her in there in the first place was because it was the only spare office they had."

I could only shake my head in wonderment.

"I can't *believe* you're serious!"

Now David was laughing.

"Cross my heart."

"But why, in heaven's name, didn't they move Elaine into one of the offices that already didn't have a door, and move one of the Senior Editors into Karen's office?"

"Because then," David explained patiently, "the *other* Senior Editors who didn't have doors would have complained."

"For God's sake, David, there are only two other Senior Editors in your department! Why don't they build each of them a door and make everybody happy?"

"Because then the Senior Editors in *your* department are

going to want doors. And the Senior Editors in the *School* Division are going to want doors. And the Senior Editors in the *Religious* Department are going to want doors."

"But, David, there can't be more than twelve Senior Editors in the whole company! How much could it possibly cost to build twelve doors?"

David shrugged. "More than they're likely to spend to make Elaine Gross happy!"

"They'd be making eleven *other* people happy, too. And they wouldn't be spending so much money. Just think of all the money they'd be saving by not *removing* doors!"

"Don't yell at me," David retorted. "This wasn't *my* idea."

Then he smiled. "Don't worry. When I get to be President of this company, you and I and Elaine and *everybody* will have a door."

I looked at him sardonically.

"David, with an attitude like that you're obviously never going to *be* President of this company!"

THIS is an extreme example of a typical corporate mindset— what I like to call the "kindergarten mentality." If a child behaved in this way, we might be able to accept it, but these are grown men and women who head major corporations. Yet their thinking is uncomfortably similar to that of the preschooler who comes home from a visit with a friend and says, "Mommy, Alice has a bigger teddy bear than I have. Mommy, can I have a teddy bear as big as Alice's?"

Mommy tries to tell her daughter that she's always *loved* her teddy bear, that she *sleeps* with her teddy bear, that Teddy would be *hurt* if she rejected him for a new bear. But the child responds churlishly, "I don't care. I don't love Teddy anymore. I want a teddy bear that's as big as Alice's."

Well, it doesn't end with kindergarten. And while Mommy, if she's wise, will discourage her child from such petty and pointless envy of other people's material possessions, the corporation will foster such jealousy among its employees, fanning the fires of envy with both hands.

One of the ploys was shown by the example of Tom in the last chapter. Tom, as you may remember, was not on a higher level than John or Jane, but he was encouraged to feel superior to them when his boss gave him the responsibility of overseeing and judging their work. All of a sudden he had a pipeline to the boss. His opinion was to be given greater weight than those of his peers. All of a sudden he was first among equals.

Well, we see that in kindergarten, too. A child, singled out to hand out the crayons or pick out the book that will be read, feels instantly superior to his friends. Woe betide the teacher who doesn't give each child a turn throughout the year. For it doesn't take much to make a child think he is better than other people. And that desire to feel superior, surely one of the nastier sides of the human psyche, is too often encouraged in business organizations.

You notice I said *feeling* superior. I am not confusing this with *being* superior, a much less nasty and much more constructive desire. *Being* superior is based on what you accomplish, not on where you stand in a hierarchy. Most normal, healthy people would dearly love—whether it is possible or not—to write better than other people, sing better than other people, even make love better than other people. Such desires, if they don't interfere with the enjoyment of the activity itself, are just fine.

And if it were *accomplishment* that the organization were solely concerned with, there would be no problem. But as often as not, employees are encouraged to compete simply for a place in the pecking order, a static position from which they may *do* great things or they may *not* do great things, but what they do is not really the point. The point is where they *are*. And how many people are looking up at them.

The concern with appearances is not limited to mere employees. Kindergarten games can be played at surprisingly high levels of power.

One such example occurred when Stuart, who was no less than Marketing Director of his company, was shown a handsome catalog of office furniture from which he could choose. Thumbing quickly through pages 13–16, which had been suggested to him, he found exactly what he wanted on page 19. "I think I'd like those," he said, pointing to several simple, but elegant, black leather chairs.

There was a moment of awkward silence. Then the Personnel Manager said in an embarrassed voice—after all, Stuart outranked and outearned him—"I'm sorry. Er, the black furnishings have been reserved for the Vice-Presidency level. I'm afraid you will have to choose between the red chairs and the blue chairs."

"But my carpet is rust!" Stuart gasped in horror.

"Yes, I see. Well, that is a problem, of course. Maybe you can get authorization from upstairs for a change in carpet. But there isn't anything I can do about getting you the black furniture. That decision has been made at the highest level." By this time it was hard to say who was the more embarrassed—Stuart or the Personnel Manager.

The end of the story? You already *know* the end of the story. Stuart wound up with blue chairs, a blue couch, and a rust-colored carpet. And, with the lights off, very late in the afternoon (in the winter, of course), it didn't look bad at all.

But the most childish example of all occurred while I was at my first job, and it occurred at the highest level in the company.

The firm was then privately owned by two men who later sold out to a huge conglomerate. They were equal partners who shared the same title—I think "President," but it might have been "Publisher" or "Chairman of the Board." It was reputed that they didn't like each other much and that they were bound together solely by their common stock. Certainly they were very different sorts of people. Petersen, who ran the business end of the operation—rather dourly, it was said by those who reported to him—was humorless, introverted, and virtually unapproachable. Rumor had it that he much preferred numbers to people, and that he had missed his vocation as a hermit. Matthews, on the other hand, who was over the editorial department, was a bon vivant with a big, booming voice. He was reputed to like, in this order, women, drink, food, golf, Broadway musicals, and entertaining celebrities.

All hell broke loose when these two mismatched partners moved their company's offices to a new building. (Why is it that all hell *always* breaks loose when companies move to different headquarters?)

Petersen and Matthews had arranged for themselves, as they had in the previous building, two enormous corner offices of exactly the same dimensions, garnering an entire city block, from 56th street to 57th street, between them. The following story was told to me by a friend of mine on the financial side:

"Did you hear that Petersen and Matthews are going to rip out the wall between their offices and rebuild it?" Jim asked me.

"They are? Why?"

"Well," Jim chuckled, "it seems the architect made a mistake. Matthews noticed that Petersen's radiator system seemed to be longer than his, so he had someone come up to measure both offices. It turned out that Petersen's office was about a foot longer than his. Matthews threw a fit and said he wouldn't stand for it and that the offices would simply have to be redone. Fortunately, they only have to knock out one wall."

"A *foot?*" I gasped. "Jim, those offices have to be thirty-five to forty feet long. What possible difference can one foot more or less make?"

Jim replied, "Those guys spend every minute of their working day making sure that neither one gets a jump on the other. Matthews was afraid that people might have drawn some unfortunate conclusions if they happened to notice that Petersen's office was even a little bit bigger."

"I very much doubt that anyone but they would have noticed," I said.

"I very much doubt it, too," said Jim.

When we see these examples of childishness taking place at the highest levels of power, we can hardly be surprised when they occur in less exalted circles. Among ourselves, to be perfectly blunt. But if we allow ourselves to become agitated and insecure when company status symbols are withheld, we are merely playing into the corporation's hands. The moral of the story? Pretend you don't care even if you do. Eventually you may find you really *don't* care. Just remember *Addison's Adage: A substantial raise in the ol' paycheck makes blue chairs on a rust carpet look perfectly elegant.* Even with the lights on.

IV
The Humiliation Trap

LET me tell you about Lester. No one ever thought Lester was shrewd, but in his own hell-bent-for-leather, crazy way, Lester may have been one of the shrewdest individuals I've ever met in any job.

Lester managed to avoid the Humiliation Trap.

He had been working for about seven years in the marketing department of the publishing house in which I was an editor. In those seven years, he had held no less than five different positions. When he screwed up one assignment, they gave him something different to do and just enough time to screw that up, too. The editorial department hated him, for they considered him the quintessential marketing type, but without the brains to know what he didn't know about books.

He didn't know anything about books.

We editors feared that Lester, because he came across as aggressive and "bottom-line" oriented, was going straight to the top of the division. From there, of course, there would have been no stopping him. No matter that he had launched projects that bombed, or meddled with projects that were enormously successful—he was "tough" and "hard-nosed" and "good with the numbers," and used the right marketing phrases. So we were worried.

Imagine our delight when a memo came around announcing that two Marketing Directors, hitherto on Lester's level, had been made divisional Vice-Presidents. Lester's name was conspicuous by its absence. What a slap in the face! What a public humiliation! We almost felt sorry for the poor bastard! Surely the embarrassment would be unbearable, and Lester would immediately begin looking for another job.

I passed Lester in the hall two days after the memo came out. I didn't know whether to look at him or look away; I could feel his humiliation acutely.

But if *Lester* felt his humiliation acutely, he didn't let on. He looked right at me, shoulders squared, and said with his customary hubris:

"I want to talk to you about the way you're pricing books. Our projections for the coming fiscal year lead me to believe that we have to raise prices rather drastically. If you can stop by my office, I'd like to talk to you about it."

Well, *there* went all the pity I had felt for Lester. Meddling around with my editorial prerogatives, as usual. Nothing had changed, goddammit!

And, of course, that's *exactly* the effect Lester wanted to have on me and on everyone else. I watched him for the next few months. He changed neither his tactics nor his demeanor. If he was upset about being passed over, he never let on. He acted as though he was delighted to have the job he had and at the company he was with. He was careful to exhibit publicly all of his usual exuberance and energy. He was his customary outrageous self at meetings.

It didn't take long for everyone to stop feeling sorry for him. Obviously, Lester, because he did not *act* humiliated, could not possibly *feel* humiliated. And since everyone knows that when you've *been* humiliated, you do indeed *feel* humiliated, the new reality of the situation was born:

Lester had not been humiliated.

By changing the perceived reality of his own situation, Lester was able to stay in the company for several more years, without everyone thinking he was an idiot for doing so. And during those next several years, the following serendipitous things happened:

One of the divisional Vice-Presidents who had been promoted over Lester was promoted again—to President of the division.

The other divisional Vice-President was given the top corporate job in a growing subsidiary of the publishing firm.

Two senior Marketing Directors, who might have been in line for a Vice-Presidency, had quit in the previous six months to take more lucrative jobs.

And suddenly, when the division found itself in the market for a Vice-President, there was . . . only *Lester!*

Well, after all, it wasn't so bad. Lester had, at one time or another, held just about every job in the department. And he had showed his loyalty to the company by staying there for ten years when he could have made more money elsewhere.

So Lester was made a Vice-President. And, if the Editorial Department believes that he has screwed up *that* job, too, the Marketing Department doesn't. Lester is doing just fine.

HERE is a potent example of the power any individual in a corporation has to make people perceive him as he wants to be perceived. This is extremely important. It is extremely necessary. Few people have a thick enough skin not to care when their peers feel sorry for them or their boss holds them in contempt. And the ability to humiliate, to cause extreme embarrassment, to make a person feel that people are talking about him unfavorably—these are among the strongest weapons in the company arsenal. Often people work their tails off just to avoid losing face. They may not especially *want* that next rung on the ladder, but they can't cope psychologically with the idea that John Doe, who has been in the company for a shorter amount of time and who started out at a much lower level, is being promoted over their heads. What will everybody think?

Well, everyone will think pretty much what you *want* them to think, depending upon how you comport yourself. There are several rules you must follow when John Doe gets his promotion.

    1. Graciously and enthusiastically praise John Doe (who may be a moron or a genius). Do it publicly, and to as many people as possible. Talk about how "perfect he is for this particular position." Indicate how hard he is going to have to work at his new job and how much you admire him

for having the stamina to take on such onerous responsibilities.

2. Indicate—subtly, of course—your immense relief at not having been asked to assume said onerous responsibilities. Indicate—also subtly—that such a burden would have (choose one or several):

a) destroyed your marriage;
b) kept you from finishing your novel;
c) threatened your relationship with your children;
d) caused your ulcer to bleed;
e) kept you from making a million dollars in real estate;
f) brought about your untimely passing.

3. Talk about how excited you are at the prospect of working with John Doe, and how perceptive the company was to see that "for that particular job, of course, he was the right person."

THERE is an even better method for avoiding humiliation than the above three rules. But in order to make it work, you must be perspicacious enough to see *in advance* that you are going to be passed over. Actually, if you are at all honest with yourself and the least bit sensitive to what is going on around you, it shouldn't really take that much perspicacity. And you don't really need to know all that *far* in advance—even a few weeks will do.

When you see that it is clear John Doe is going to get the top job—even if you happen to want it—this is what you must do:

Tell as many people as you can—in "the strictest confidence," of course, that you have figured out that John Doe will be promoted to Director of Operational Procedures for Systems Analysis. Say that this would be *your* decision if you had the power to make that decision, and that you are sure that the powers-that-be will be smart enough to see that John is the right person for that particular job. If someone is complimentary enough to say he thinks *you* will—or should—get the job, you just smile knowingly, and say: "Thanks, but I really don't think I'd be right for it, and anyway Jones already knows I don't want it." You can then mention the onerous responsibilities, your devotion to your children, or your bleeding ulcer, but in this case, you can hardly be accused of sour grapes, since the thing has not yet happened.

When it *does* happen, you buttonhole all the people with whom you already have shared your prediction:

"See," you gasp excitedly, "I was right! John got the director-ship! What did I tell you! I've seen that coming for a long time."

What you have done is to shift the focus of attention from your failure to land the directorship to your unique gifts as a soothsayer. People will then discuss you in the following man-ner: "Jack knew all along that Jones would make John Doe Director. No one else would have guessed it." And suddenly, al-though you may not be a Director, you have become a Canny Person. And if someone should blurt out, "But didn't Jack want that job himself?" there are twenty people to tell him: "No. He told me weeks ago, and in the strictest confidence, that he wanted enough free time to finish that novel he's writing."

A sense of humor can also be a potent defense against corpo-rate humiliation. Joyce, who works for a Senior Editor recently passed over for promotion to Managing Editor, told me about Alan's crack to her:

"We were discussing a manuscript about women who get ahead by balling their way to the top. I told Alan, facetiously, of course, that perhaps instead of working these long, hard hours, I should simply have an affair with him. 'Right,' he said, without missing a beat, 'you can ball your way to the *middle!*' " The story got around the office, and everyone laughed. *With* Alan, not *at* him. And people who hadn't known what to say to Alan in the light of his terrible public humiliation were comfortable with him once again.

THE problem of coping with corporate humiliation is one that men have been wrestling with since the invention of corpora-tions. But it is a relatively new problem for women.

Until recently—more specifically, until the women's move-ment and the ERA—women, no matter what their ability and ambition, had precious little chance of rising higher than a certain level in the corporate world. A few extraordinary ones did, of course, but they were the exceptions. Not only were women not expected to rise very high, but they were not expected to want to. A woman of greater-than-average ambition often had to apologize for that ambition—it was "peculiar" and, some thought, "unfeminine." So that when Jane Doe was passed over for a younger, less experienced male, it was thought to be in the nature of things.

There were two edges to that sword. The bad edge, as we all know, is that Jane Doe was denied equal opportunity under the law. But the good edge was that Jane, if she really didn't hunger after enormous power and glory, didn't have to feel guilty or unworthy. The rules were imposed from the outside, and she had society to blame for her lack of advancement.

Now, as Jane watches younger, less experienced *women* being promoted over her head, she feels she has no one to blame but herself. She *should* want more power. She *should* want to manage other people. And if she doesn't, someone else will be catapulted right past her. Not necessarily a man, either.

I have talked with many young, able women who feel these new pressures acutely. One of them, Linda, who works in the publicity department of a major publishing house, had some interesting things to say:

"You know, sometimes I almost wish I had started here twenty years ago. I wouldn't have gotten to a top executive level to be sure, but I think I could have made it to my present position. I enjoy my job. It's stimulating, I travel a lot, and I meet a lot of interesting people. The next step is administrative, and frankly I don't really want it. I wouldn't be able to travel nearly as much, and I'd be dealing more with paperwork than with people."

"So why take it?" I asked.

She sighed.

"I'm thirty-three years old, and I've been here six years. There's a twenty-seven-year-old hot-shot financial prodigy named Nancy who is already a divisional Vice-President. She's only been here two years, for God's sake, and she's accomplished much more than I have. If she were a *man*, I might be able to rationalize the situation, but how can you rationalize a twenty-seven-year-old *female* Vice-President?"

"You can't rationalize it," I answered. "You can only decide what *you* want out of life."

Linda looked unconvinced.

"That's why I told you I wished I'd begun working twenty years ago. Sometimes I'm terribly envious of Dorothy."

"Who's Dorothy?" I asked.

"Dorothy works in the department and is on my level. She's been here for almost twenty years and will forget more about dealing with media people and arranging author tours than most people will ever know. She is extremely highly regarded; all the other departments come to her about virtually everything.

"She adores her job. I think she's pretty well paid, too. Everyone treats her with the utmost respect. She gets to travel. And she isn't at all uncomfortable about not being an executive. You see, by the standards of publishing that existed when she first entered, she's gone as high as any woman could go. She's pleased with her position. She *feels* like a success.

"So she's lucky. She has all the advantages of a job she loves with none of the hang-ups *I* have when younger people get promoted to high positions. She's at peace with herself."

And what will Linda, who is not at peace with herself, do? I asked her.

"I don't know. Honest to God, I don't know. If somebody were to offer me that next promotion, I frankly don't know if I'd have the guts to turn it down."

"It really matters to you what other people think?"

She looked at me with an absolutely miserable expression on her face.

"Yes," she said. "It matters terribly."

LINDA is a victim of the Humiliation Trap. Probably she will be offered that promotion to an administrative level. Probably she will take it. And the likelihood is that she will then be, as she now fears she *will* be, less happy than she is now. But she will be able to hold her head up high: she will be a "success." And surely that is more important than mere happiness.

Or is it? For an impassioned defense of mere happiness, please turn to the next chapter.

V

In Defense of Hedonism

HEDONISM has a bad name. The word, usually employed too narrowly, conjures up images of naked men and women cavorting on a tropical beach; fathers abandoning their children to sail around the world in a twelve-foot boat; hippies sniffing cocaine in Haight-Ashbury while they stubbornly refuse to "get an honest job."

Nonsense! Some of the most productive, self-actualizing people I have ever known have been hedonists, while some of the most neurotic, self-defeating individuals have swallowed the Protestant Ethic whole and nearly choked on it.

Hedonism and achievement are not mutually exclusive. It is perfectly possible to pursue the greatest happiness for oneself within the structure of a forty-hour work week. In fact, it is my thesis that hedonism and achievement make happy bedfellows indeed.

My defense of the hedonistic approach stems from the following axiom:

You know whether or not you are happy today. You cannot be sure, no matter what you may do today, whether or not you will be happy tomorrow.

Let us look at the travails of a determined nonhedonist. Ben is a close friend of mine, even though we are two very different sorts of people. He tolerantly forgives my "live for today" attitude and I good-naturedly overlook his insistence on the necessity for "personal growth" within a job. Ben gets bored if he is too comfortable or happy; I get anxious and irritable if I am not.

Until recently, Ben was with a small publishing house specializing in "coffee table" books. He worked for a boss he very much liked and who liked him. His boss had been handling a certain procedural task that was highly important but extremely dull. Ben was given a choice of whether he wanted to assume that task or not; his boss realized it was dull and exacting and did not insist on saddling Ben with it.

Ben knew it was an area he didn't much want to get into. But because he thought it was "good for him" to learn about it, and because he thought that by pleasing the boss his future was assured, he took it on. He did the job well and conscientiously, and his boss was indeed pleased.

Five months later, however, his boss left to take another job. The new man who came in didn't like Ben, and the feeling was mutual. Ben was summarily fired.

None of this could have been foreseen, of course. And it might never have happened. But Ben, in spite of doing something to get ahead, even something he didn't enjoy, was at the mercy of circumstances beyond his control.

I put it to him, after he was happily ensconced in a new job, that the five months spent on a boring, exhausting task might have been avoided. But Ben is incorrigible. He doesn't have a hedonistic bone in his body.

"Oh sure," he said. "But it was valuable for me to have had that experience."

I asked him if he ever wanted to have that experience in the future.

"No," he answered. "But anything new you learn is valuable. It's helpful for personal growth."

I just coughed. He laughed.

"OK, OK. But remember, folks like me who think that way make it possible for people like you to avoid dull tasks."

I laughed then, too, as I thought of all the ambitious people in my own department who had volunteered for boring assignments I didn't want to touch.

Had their sacrifices gotten them ahead?

In some cases, yes; in some cases, no. But the irony was that in the two cases I could think of where the people *had* been promoted as a reward for the unpleasant responsibilities they had assumed, they were both then stuck with those assignments as their grand new levels. They continued to do the same dull work, but with a better title, and with, one assumes, higher pay. (This is only an assumption; companies often give titles in lieu of higher pay.) And they were the *lucky* ones. Several other people who took on tasks no one else wanted to assume were not promoted; they were so valuable doing the thankless tasks that the boss wanted them to stay right where they were.

The moral of the story: Pick out those responsibilities you think you will *enjoy*. If you bring enthusiasm and ebullience to your job, you will make a good impression. If you make a good impression, you may well be promoted. If you fail to be promoted, you will still have a good time. And if something unforeseen goes wrong, such as the sort of thing that happened to Ben, you will then have nothing to be bitter about, and you will be able to be philosophical about the vicissitudes of life.

But, you may ask, can a hedonist ever achieve corporate success?

You'd better believe it! Let me give you an example of a hedonistic super-achiever.

I always knew Wendy was brilliant, hard-working, well-organized, disciplined, and calm-in-a-crisis. I always knew she'd go far. And she did. Today, Wendy is one of the two dozen or so top women in the publishing industry. She heads the editorial department of a major hardcover house.

Wendy and I have been friends since our early years, working together in my first job. And in all that time, I never once thought of her as hedonistic. Far from it. In addition to being an achiever, Wendy is a WASP from a small town in New England. Discipline runs in her blood and positively gallops through her veins. I don't think she has ever slept later than eight o'clock in the morning. She works long days, takes work home at night, and juggles responsibilities that would stagger an army. She is also one of the world's nicest human beings and one of the most forthright. Her staff adores her.

When I decided to leave my own job to write this book—something all editors dream of doing—I spoke to Wendy, who had done just that. During the two-year stint between her last terrific publishing job and her current terrific publishing job, Wendy had written not one, but two fine novels, both of which had been published, both of which had received impressive reviews. Wendy had achieved this in her usual disciplined way, never rising after eight A.M., writing every day, without fail, from nine to one.

Less disciplined than Wendy, I was fashioning my writing schedule around my tennis schedule, meaning that I only worked during rainstorms, hailstorms, 100-degree heat waves, fire and brimstone, and when the temperature dropped below 45 degrees. Sometimes I wrote in the morning, sometimes in the evening, and sometimes—dare I admit it?—I didn't write at all.

Nevertheless, I was having a wonderful time, and found that my days were busy and full. I told Wendy that I was surprised at how few hours there seemed to be in a day, and said I thought I could keep up this lifestyle for at least six months without feeling the need to go back to a more structured way of life.

"Be careful," she warned. "It can be infecting."

I thought I knew what she meant.

"You mean that once I'm out of work for six months, I may *never* want to go back!"

She smiled.

"No. What I'm saying is that once you've been out for a while and you've *gone* back, it's always in the back of your mind that you can do it again."

I looked at her in amazement. Surely with her current terrific publishing job, she wasn't thinking along those lines. Not Wendy! Of all people! Heavens!

She could see I was surprised. And then she shared with me a secret that I was sure she hadn't shared with many other people.

"I was out of work for almost two years," she said. *"And it was very nice.* So when things get a little too hectic or frustrating, I think to myself that I did it once, and I can always do it again."

She laughed.

"I told you it was infecting."

Suddenly I saw brilliant, successful, motivated, disciplined Wendy in a whole new light.

"Wendy," I said, "you're nothing but a bloody hedonist like me!"

"You're right," she replied. "But I'm not sure I'd spread it around."

As can be seen, Wendy has accomplished more, both inside and outside the corporation, in just a few years than many people do in a lifetime. But she is not driven by a need to achieve. She maintains a sense of humor and an awareness of life's absurdities. Refusing to become caught up in the trappings of power and status, she retains the option of giving them up when the desire for a different experience strikes her. I would argue that it is this essentially hedonistic attitude that gives Wendy the energy to accomplish so much.

But were you to meet Wendy, you would never think of her as anything but a super-achiever. She hides that healthy streak of hedonism very well indeed.

VI
It Is Lonely at the Top

So you agree you want to be happy. But why, you ask, can't you be happy in a high-paying, high-status job and possess, in addition to your happiness, a country chateau, a Rolls-Royce, a private tennis court, and a house full of servants?

Well, you *can*. But chances are that the high-paying, high-status job will be an administrative one. There are few instances of lucrative corporate jobs that are not administrative; and while, for example, you can make a fortune if you are a doctor by doing what you entered the profession to do in the first place, practice medicine, in the corporate world the people making enormous money doing what they originally wanted to do are rare:

- The advertising copywriter who loves the creative process is underpaid until he becomes an account executive.

- The architect who loves to design buildings leaves a large firm because he is underpaid and can't get a partnership. He starts his own architectural firm, eventually has ten people working for him, and becomes inextricably involved with legal contracts, rental overhead, profit and loss statements, and personnel problems. Precious little time is left for designing buildings; his staff does that.

- The biochemist, who hopes to discover a cure for cancer, is so well regarded that he is put in charge of the Foundation Research Institute. What with the fund-raising forays to Washington, the endless reports that must be written up, and the organization of research teams, the poor biochemist is lucky if he gets to spend fifteen hours a week in the lab. Now he's making big money and has an impressive title, but secretly he yearns to get back to the microscope.

This is the great dilemma—one that every ambitious person must confront. You must ask yourself: Do I want to be an administrator? That's where the money is. That's where the status is. But will I enjoy the *process* of managing other people?

If you decide you will, be prepared for some very sticky situations. At an administrative level, the pressure to play corporate games becomes almost unbearable. You are now—at least to the people who report to you—the *voice* of the corporation. One of your main responsibilities will be to impose policies arrived at by your superiors on your staff. Often you will not agree with those policies. But it is not considered good managerial form to say so.

Let's see how good a manager you would make. Here's another quiz for you to try your hand at. Pick the answer that comes *closest* to what you would do in these ten difficult situations.

QUIZ NUMBER TWO

1. A stupid, pointless, and officious memo is circulated by the Personnel Department. A subordinate, who happens to be a close friend of yours, jocularly tells you that the memo proves what he's known all along: that Personnel Departments are stupid, pointless, and officious, and that the one in *your* company really takes the cake. Your response:
   a) Your subordinates are *never* "close friends."
   b) You say: "This is the stupidest memo they've come up with in the fifteen years I've been here."
   c) You say: "I'm having some problems with this memo, too, but I'm afraid we will all have to go along with it."
   d) You say: "I think these new rules will make the company work more smoothly, and I expect your full cooperation."

2. Your most productive subordinate is going through a divorce. She tries to give the job her full attention, but ses-

sions with her lawyer and emotional trauma are causing her to slack off from time to time. You:

a) Say nothing; it's a legitimate problem, and she's earned a little leeway.

b) Tell her you understand what she's going through, but that her job will have to come first.

c) Tell her you understand what she's going through, but that you hope she will make an "extra effort" since the department is short-handed.

d) Tell her you are displeased: you assumed she was a professional, and that personal problems must simply not interfere with her work.

3. There is one empty office, and two members of your staff, now in cubicles, with equal claim to it. You:

a) Tell the candidates that they both have equal claim, and that you are therefore going to draw straws.

b) Leave the office empty for a few months. Tell the two candidates that you will be watching to see who you think is the more deserving.

c) Leave the office empty for a few months but say nothing. The two candidates will work their tails off, because they *assume* you will be watching them.

d) Give the office to the wheel that squeaks the loudest.

4. There is a limited amount of money to cover raises for your staff this year. You:

a) Divide it equally among everyone, thus making everyone somewhat happy.

b) Give significant raises to your most valuable people; token raises to the rest.

c) Give major raises to your most valuable people; no raises at all to everyone else.

d) Give minor raises where you must give raises; no raises where you can get away with it. The less money for your staff, the more money is left for *you*.

5. Your boss is looking to you for major innovations in the department. You have a subordinate who has been doing things the same way for ten years. His projects are enormously successful; you know there is no reason for him to

change his *modus operandi*. But you are being judged for your ability to turn things around. You:

a) Tell him he's been doing things the same way for ten years, and that, damn it, you want some innovations.

b) Tell him you would be interested in hearing any new ideas he has for his projects.

c) Tell him that the boss seems to want innovations for the sake of innovations, but that you and he had better come up with something—*anything*—quick!

d) Suggest some new ideas that you have for his projects, and ask him to give you his best opinion as to whether or not they will work.

6. You are told that you and your staff have two weeks to implement a new program. You know two weeks are insufficient and that your department would virtually have to work around the clock to complete it in that time. You tell your boss:

a) "That's not enough time to get the job done, and I can't ask my people to do something infeasible."

b) "I can't promise the outstanding job I would like to do for you in just two weeks. But allow me four weeks and I'm sure I can come up with one hell of a program."

c) "I'll do the best I can. But I can't vouch for the ability of my staff to measure up to such a critical assignment in so short a time."

d) "It will be done. I may have to drive my people unmercifully, but I won't let you down."

7. Let us assume you have promised the boss to crash through that new program in two weeks. You tell your staff:

a) "The company's being pretty unreasonable about this. I don't see what the big rush is. But it's got to be done, so let's all pitch in and help, shall we?"

b) "I told Mr. Jones I had a superb staff, and that if any department in the company could get the job done, you could."

c) "My ass is on the line. So if you want me to be around for a while, you'll have to make a heroic effort, each and every one of you."

d) "I don't want to hear any griping. This is the nature of

the job, and anyone who feels he can't devote the extra time had better start looking for another job."

8. You are getting flak from the Personnel Department because a sizable number of people in your department don't get in on time in the morning. You have overlooked this because you know that they all stay late and they all take work home on a regular basis. Furthermore, you are pleased with the amount of work they produce, and you know the morale is high. You tell Personnel:
   a) All of the above, and sweetly suggest they overlook the late mornings, too.
   b) That their department should be half as productive as yours, and that hours, *per se,* do not remotely interest you.
   c) That you will try to get your people in earlier, but that old habits die hard, and only limited success can be expected.
   d) That you have already spoken to your staff about your displeasure, and that sterner measures will now be forthcoming.

9. You address your staff as follows about those late mornings:
   a) "I want you in at 9:00—no ands, ifs, or buts."
   b) "I know 9:00 is ridiculously early, but 10:00 is too late. Please be in by 9:30."
   c) "I know you all stay late and take work home, but the company does have regulations. Therefore, I'm afraid you are going to have to come in earlier."
   d) "That idiotic Personnel Department seems to have nothing better to do than conduct bed-checks. Look, can you just come in earlier for a few weeks and at least get them off my back for the time being?"

10. You absolutely cannot get a raise this year for someone who has assumed no new responsibilities. You fought the good fight, and you like her and want her to stay, but the limited salary budget went into raises for the two people who were promoted. You handle the situation this way:
    a) You tell her you tried, but failed, and that you're very sorry, but you hope she will be patient enough to wait until next year when you will be able to get a raise through.

b) You tell her you will fabricate some "new responsibilities" for her, and that you should then be able to get her a raise in three months.

c) You tell her: "I'm afraid I cannot see my way clear to giving you a raise this year, since you are doing the same job you were doing a year ago."

d) You say nothing: she's a very insecure person, and won't have the guts to come to you about it. Nor will she have the guts to look for another job.

Scoring

Award yourself the following number of points for each answer:

Question 1: a–3; b–0; c–1; d–2
Question 2: a–0; b–2; c–1; d–3
Question 3: a–1; b–2; c–3; d–0
Question 4: a–0; b–1; c–2; d–3
Question 5: a–3; b–1; c–0; d–2
Question 6: a–0; b–1; c–2; d–3
Question 7: a–0; b–2; c–1; d–3
Question 8: a–1; b–0; c–2; d–3
Question 9: a–3; b–1; c–2; d–0
Question 10: a–0; b–1; c–3; d–2

Evaluation

Score 0–8 points: You are a real soft touch and had better put any dreams of management right out of your head. It is not possible for you to implement policies with which you don't agree, and you're *surely* not going to play the heavy in such cases. Being liked is much more important to you than getting the job done, and you basically want to be "just one of the guys." Your subordinates would love you, but some of them might be tempted to walk all over you, too. And if the company was misguided enough to give you an administrative job in the first place (they probably wouldn't), then they would see the error of their ways within a matter of months, and take remedial action.

Score 9–21 points: You possess a certain cleverness and imaginativeness in walking the tightrope between being fair and reasonable with your subordinates and getting things done. You are the kind of person who would be both loved and respected as a supervisor. Indeed, you are the sort of person that you, yourself, would like to work for. The problem is that your basic decency, honesty, and sense of fair play will make an administrative job painful for you. You will experience a great many tension-producing conflicts, where you feel you're damned if you do, and damned if you don't. You will be tempted to confide your dilemmas to your subordinates much more often than is prudent. Because you can't quite bring yourself to badmouth the system when you know the system *deserves* to be badmouthed, you are going to feel isolated and lonely much of the time. In short, your subordinates will thrive and you will suffer. Eventually, you may simply have to remove yourself from the daily conflicts by quitting, thus abandoning your staff to a less soft-hearted, less decent supervisor than yourself.

Score 22–30 points: I hope I shall never have to work for you, my friend! You bill yourself as a "tough boss" and take pride in same. No conflicts for you when you assume power! You know how to look in only one direction—*up.* If your next promotion necessitates bullying your staff, treating them shabbily, or even driving them to early graves, so be it. The more you are hated, the better you feel you are doing your job. Your great value to the organization is that you have no compunction whatever about shouldering the blame for even their most outrageous policies. But you are not nearly as effective a manager as you may think: Your subordinates are spending virtually the entire working day protecting their collective flanks; what little energy is left over is spent thinking how they can murder you and get away with it!

So now you know whether or not you are cut out for a managerial post. But the purpose of the quiz was also to illustrate the sorts of problems—often exceedingly unpleasant—that administrators face every day.

Bill, a biochemist who is the husband of a publishing friend of mine, was mentioned earlier in the chapter. He is easygoing and low-keyed—so nice, in fact, that his wife almost doesn't know how to deal with it.

"I guess I'm sort of a feminist," Jeanne told me, "and certainly all my women friends are. Most of them are single or divorced or in the process of getting a divorce, and they kid me all the time about my marriage. They all say I surely can't be as happily married as I pretend to be."

She looked almost guilty about it.

"But I *am*, I tell them. How can I not be? I have such a *nice* husband! I tell them I don't *deserve* Bill—I'm not nearly as nice as he is! I'm neurotic and insecure and driven, and I'm going to a shrink, and throughout it all, Bill remains his supportive, good-humored self. I never had a *roommate* who was so easy to get along with."

Then she added:

"He's not only nice to me. He's a really nice guy at work, too. And that's why he can't deal with the problems of being an administrator."

I asked Jeanne if I could talk to Bill about his job. I told her I was writing a book.

"I'm sure he'd love to talk to you," she said.

I spoke to Bill one evening as he was relaxing over an iced-tea after work. Such a likable, well-adjusted guy, and he doesn't even drink!

"This management thing sort of crept up on me when I wasn't looking," Bill began. "It seems one minute I was involved in my own research into cellular behavior, and the next thing I knew, I had forty scientists working for me, not to mention the responsibility for scrounging new government funding once every two years.

"The whole thing is a terrible headache. For one thing, we

have an important cancer research program, and if it isn't re-funded, the possibility of finding a cure in our lifetime is that much more reduced.

"But there's more to it than that. The forty people who work for me all have families and responsibilities. If the institute is closed down, they are going to be out on the street. There simply aren't that many research programs in the country, and there are a great number of scientists involved in the field. Everyone with the appropriate scientific background wants to be the one to discover a cure for cancer."

He shifted in his chair.

"So I worry. I worry chronically that the money won't be forthcoming, and that I'll be the one who has to break it to the team that their jobs have vanished. And I worry that it will be my fault—that someone who was more of a PR type or a more eloquent speaker might have convinced Washington to continue the program when I couldn't.

"I'm really not very good at that sort of thing, you know. I'm not terribly verbal or persuasive. You might say I'm a typical scientist: more comfortable looking through a microscope than talking to people."

I said he seemed pretty comfortable talking to me.

"It's different," he replied. "I can just say whatever comes into my head with you. Talking to government officials is hardly the same thing. I tense up and forget what I want to say. Or else I use scientific terminology that goes right over their heads. A different sort of person would do much better in these circumstances, perhaps someone who was not a scientist at all."

I tried to assure him that he was putting himself down for no reason. "After all," I said, "you've gotten the program re-funded twice already."

"Well, come next January, I'll tell you whether I've been putting myself down unnecessarily, or not."

I asked him how he felt about having so much less time for actual experiments in the lab.

"Maybe that's the worst part of the whole thing," he answered. "I have almost no time to do my own experiments.

"If our institute succeeds in coming up with a discovery that proves important in finding a cure for cancer, someone else on the team will make it, not me."

I told him that I could well appreciate the glory of going down in history as the person who discovered the cure for cancer, and that I could understand his hunger to be that person. He laughed.

"Spoken like a true nonscientist," he responded lightly. "That's what all laymen think, and that's why they wouldn't make very good researchers."

"What do you mean?" I asked.

"To the pure scientist, what is interesting is the problem itself. You probably think I went into cancer research out of an enormous need to save mankind. Right?"

"Right," I agreed.

"I went into cancer research because the *challenge* appealed to me. Here's a problem no one's been able to crack. Thousands of talented people working on it, and we still don't know much more than we ever did. To a biochemist, it's about the thorniest problem around, and that's why so many people have gone into it.

"Anyway, my job has become so damned administrative, that it almost wouldn't matter if the institute was doing research in plastics. I don't even *see* a frozen cell section from one end of the week to another."

"But you couldn't go *backward*, could you?" I asked. "I mean, after running the whole show, you couldn't just be another scientist in the lab?"

Bill looked over at Jeanne.

"Sure, I could. I think more and more about it every day. I could live on a lot less than I'm making now. I've got my kids in public schools, the apartment's rent controlled, and neither Jeanne nor I is extravagant by nature.

"I'll tell you this much. If the program doesn't get re-funded in January, I won't take another job of this kind. Either I'll work as a researcher in another foundation, or I'll go into teaching."

"And if the program *does* get re-funded?"

Bill sighed.

"Then I guess I'll have to see it through, at least for the next two years."

BILL is not unique. When I mentioned this book to various friends, I found myself inundated with stories of people who were unhappy in administrative positions.

One individual told me to talk to her younger brother, a lawyer with a civil liberties organization.

Jason was only twenty-seven, but was already involved in a career in the more glamorous, social-minded (and less lucrative) aspects of the law. After making Law Review at Harvard, he had clerked for two years for a Federal Judge in Philadelphia, a plum assignment that every young lawyer dreams of, but few are fortunate enough to land. Then he had gotten a position that sounded equally glamorous and influential: he was a staff lawyer with a civil liberties organization, involved in just that field which most appealed to him—what he called "social impact law."

But he wasn't happy.

"I don't do any lawyering," Jason explained. "My job is two-fold: 1) to decide which cases the organization will and won't handle, and 2) to assign the appropriate case to an appropriate lawyer from our bulging files.

"I spend the whole day on the phone. I *hate* the phone! I've *always* hated the phone!

"I don't do any litigation myself. I've never taken a case to court. That isn't my job. The closest I come to arguing a case is to tell the lawyer I've assigned to it the tack that our office feels he should take in litigating it."

Jason made an impatient gesture.

"I feel like a horse's ass! Imagine, a snot-nosed twenty-seven year old kid, who's never even *been* in court, telling experienced lawyers of forty or fifty how they should present their cases. These guys I assign to take cases to court have argued hundreds of cases. I've never argued one."

Jason shook his head.

"I tell you, I feel like an idiot."

He went on:

"My supervisor has been doing this same job for fifteen years. I'm not sure he's ever litigated a case himself. I'm not sure he'd even know how! But he loves the administrative end of it. Maybe it makes him feel important, I don't know."

Then he leaned back in his chair and seemed to relax a bit.

"I'm being unfair. Actually, Charles is very good at his job. He's extremely well organized and detail-minded, and he can juggle a lot of balls at the same time. The organization is lucky to have him—he makes things run smoothly. And maybe he has a lot more talent as an administrator than he would have had as a litigator.

"But that's not true of me. I went into law to *practice* law! I never went into court as a clerk, I merely helped prepare the briefs. And I don't go into court now. But so help me, my next job—I'm quitting this one in June—my next job, I'm going to do some *lawyering*, for a change."

Jason's situation is highly unusual. Most people get thrust into administration *after* they have proven themselves in their respective fields. Jason landed in administration before he had proven himself in his chosen field, and this led him to doubt not only his desire to be an administrator, but also his competence.

I was strongly impressed by Jason. His humility and sense of his own absurdity in presuming to tell far more experienced lawyers how to present cases in court seemed unusual in a young man of twenty-seven. How many others might have let it go to their heads, grooved on the power trip, and become petty executives?

One final example of an individual who found herself misplaced in an administrative role. Unlike Bill or Jason, Connie has already acted upon the decision to get out of it. To the outside observer, she has "gone backward." To her own way of thinking, she has made a sensible and necessary decision, one that she doesn't regret at all.

Connie was Editorial Director of a high-powered paperback publishing house. Twenty people reported to her; she had control over acquisition money (in the millions of dollars), expense accounts (not quite in the millions of dollars) and salaries (certainly *not* in the millions of dollars!). For five years she wielded as much power as anyone in publishing. And the "perks" were terrific: business lunches at the best restaurants every day; hobnobbing with the rich and famous at glamorous parties; "working" vacations in Jamaica and the Bahamas. Not to mention a hefty salary.

At the end of five years, Connie abruptly quit her job. She took a year off to unwind—fortunately she had no dependents to support—and then she began to look for another job. As might be imagined, the offers that flooded in were of a high administrative sort: She hadn't been happy as an Editorial Director? So maybe she'd like a Vice-Presidency?

Connie turned them all down. And in so doing, she made it abundantly clear to her publishing associates that what she really wanted was to be a Senior Editor.

Her publishing associates were shocked.

"But that's not a *big* enough job for you, Connie," they protested.

She just laughed.

"I don't have to *have* the biggest publishing job in New York," she answered. "I've done all that. Now I just want to get back to books. Maybe even have my own imprint."

She paused.

"Do any of you *know* of a house that would give me my own imprint?"

It took six months. But Connie now has her own imprint.

I asked Connie some pointed questions at a recent publishing lunch. I wasn't sure she'd answer them—I don't know her especially well—but she was surprisingly forthcoming.

"I think I was a masochist to stay in that job for five years," she declared. "You know it's an old cliché, but it really is true."

"What is?"

"It's *lonely* at the top. And the higher you get, the lonelier it seems to be."

I asked her to explain. I knew that I felt that way, but Connie, after all, had handled the job successfully for a long time. Obviously she wouldn't have lasted if she hadn't had some administrative capabilities.

Many of the things she told me became the inspiration for the quiz earlier in the chapter. They were real horror stories about trying to balance a commitment to your staff against a commitment to top management.

"It can't be done," she said. "You end up screwing one or angering the other. It's an endless tightrope.

"And that's only the ethical side of it. On the practical side is the never-ending paperwork—boring, officious stuff that has to be done, and it can't be done by anyone but you. That—and the meetings."

"I go to meetings," I interjected.

"So maybe you go to two meetings a week. By the last year I was there I was going to two meetings a *day*. Not meetings with other editors or with authors. Meetings with salesmen, and marketing directors, and data processing people, and computer programmers, and financial analysts, and heaven knows who else. Most meetings are colossal wastes of time. These were no exception, and they were boring, besides. And I didn't have the time to devote to them. I had to do all my editorial work at home, and ended giving up all my evenings and all my weekends. Except, of course, when I was too upset to work, because I was worrying that I couldn't get Bob a raise or Sally an office."

She ordered the rack of lamb—rare. Even at her reduced status, Connie still enjoyed a lot of her previous "perks."

"My advice to you," she said, "is don't let yourself be talked into that kind of job. You seem to have a nice life. Go *on* having a nice life."

More wine arrived, and by now Connie was pretty well lubricated.

"Look," she said, "in a way I'm glad I did it. The money was good, and now I'm in the position of not having any real financial worries.

"So I have peace of mind. I'm working with books and authors again. Someone else can tell Sally that she'll have to remain in her five-foot by seven-foot cubicle. Someone else will have to tell Bob that there isn't enough money in the coffers for even a minimal raise. And someone else can give up his—or her—weekends, evenings, vacations, and all the rest.

"My life is manageable again. I have time for myself and for the projects that give me pleasure. I worked for it, and I deserve it!"

I told Connie that I admired her for being a person with both the ability to get to the top and the courage to walk away from it.

"Courage?" she said, and laughed. "Are you kidding? I just decided I didn't want to drop dead in my forties of some stress-related illness.

"Do you know when and where I made the decision to get out of management? It was a snap decision, and I made it lying flat on my back on a mattress on the floor of the Manor House Lodge at a mountain retreat in the Poconos."

"You were on vacation at the time?" I asked.

"Hell, no!" Connie said. "I was at a 'Stress Management Clinic' that my company was paying for me to attend to the tune of three hundred dollars a day for three days. A lot of companies have started similar programs for their top executives, and it's because, we were told, stress-related disorders cost American industry perhaps as much as fifty million dollars each year in absenteeism, serious illness, alcoholism, drug abuse, and so forth. I don't know how concerned they are with us as people, but when job performance is adversely affected, companies will spend huge sums of money to try and improve it.

"I had complained of migraines, which are definitely caused by tension, so the company packed me off to the Poconos where supposedly I would learn to 'manage' my stress.

"The people at the clinic, successful as they might have been—and they turned out to be some of the top executives on the East Coast—all sounded like the walking wounded when you talked to them. Several had had heart attacks and all the rest had symptoms ranging from peptic ulcers to backaches to high blood pressure. But they were all optimistic about learning new techniques to cope 'more creatively' with pressure. And they all felt that their respective companies were doing something really terrific for them by sending them to the retreat at such great expense.

"Anyway, there I was lying on a mattress on the floor between an overweight automobile tycoon and an asthmatic television bigwig, and this disembodied voice out of a tape recorder was saying: 'I'd like you to visualize that you're out in a beautiful meadow. It's a lovely spring day. You can feel the warmth of the sun on your face and body. You can smell the flowers. You can hear the silence. Now, take a nice, deep breath,' and say the word "relax." Exhale slowly. You can feel yourself going limp . . .'

"At those words, every muscle in my body stiffened in rebellion as the absurdity of the situation suddenly became clear to me. My God! It *was* spring outside. There *were* flowers! There *was* a meadow! There was real silence, too—not some irritating voice coming out of a machine. And I knew I wanted to *be* outside, not stuck in this airless, musty room with a lot of other hypertense executives.

"But here's the thing. At just that moment, I also realized that I didn't want to learn how to 'manage' my stress. I wanted to get rid of it entirely! More precisely, I wanted to get rid of the job pressures that were causing it. And within three weeks of my return from Manor House Lodge, I had given the company notice."

She chuckled. "I didn't have the heart to tell them that the clinic was what made me decide to quit. After all, it cost them almost a thousand dollars to send me there!"

"Anyway," she concluded, "it was the right decision for me to make, and, as I said before, I'm happier than I've been in a long time. And best of all, my migraines have disappeared completely."

"To your continued good health," I said, clinking my wine glass against hers.

"And yours," she toasted back.

"And to the health of everyone who was at the stress clinic

that weekend," I said in a burst of altruistic concern, taking another sip.

"And to everyone who wasn't, but should have been," Connie added generously.

And then we each ordered another glass of wine. All in the interest of good health, of course.

VII

How to Turn Down a Promotion

NOT many people could do what Connie did. It is hard to give up a high-status job for one of lower status. You worry that people are talking about you behind your back, and that what they are saying is not flattering: "Didn't have the stuff, you know." "Don't know how he lasted as long as he did in a big job like that." "I always knew she was in over her head."

You may protest as much as you like that what you are now doing is a great deal more rewarding than that "big job" you gave up—there will always be some people who don't believe you.

And there's another problem. While you were in that high-status, probably high-paying job, you and your family will have become accustomed to a lifestyle that you will no longer be able to maintain. It is harder to give up comforts and luxuries that you once had than never to have had them in the first place.

Therefore: *Steele's Law No. 1:*

It is easier never to go forward than to have to go backward.

And, *Steele's Corollary No. 1a:*

Therefore, you will have to learn how to turn down promotions.

Turning down a promotion is one of the most delicate and potentially dangerous things you will ever have to do in an office. Which leads to:

Steele's Corollary No. 1b:

It is better to make sure you are never offered a promotion you don't want than to have to turn it down.

The behavior you should ideally follow to make sure you are not offered said promotion is remarkably similar to the advice offered in Chapter IV on dealing with being passed over.

You must ascertain *in advance* if there is any unwanted assignment with which you are about to be honored. If you think there is, you must leak to as many of your peers as possible, "in the strictest confidence," of course, that you would not want said honor, that you feel you would handle it badly, that your boss would be making a mistake by giving it to you. You then tell your confidant:

"On the other hand, *you* would be really terrific as Executive Managing Director of Traffic Flow and Inventory. You're so much better organized than I am. And everyone respects you so much."

Make sure that at least one person you confide in hates your guts and/or himself wants to be Executive Managing Director of Traffic Flow and Inventory. He's your best bet to leak your confidence; the others are added insurance.

If this ploy fails—and it may—you will then have to take the risk of telling your boss that you do not want the golden opportunity he is thrusting upon you with eager hands. As I said, this is very delicate. Your boss may feel he needs you in that post. He may not trust anyone else to handle it. Or—far more insidious—he may know that nobody in his right mind *wants* to be Executive Managing Director of Traffic Flow and Inventory, and may be sticking you with the job to force you to resign, for some ulterior motive of his own.

If this latter is true, forget it. You've bought the course, and you might as well look for another job. Your boss has it in for you, and there isn't much you can do about it.

But if your boss really thinks he is doing you a favor; if he feels that the Executive Managing Directorship is the most splendid gift boss can offer employee, you will have to take a fairly careful and subtle tack.

1. Thank him profusely and gratefully for the enormous confidence he has shown in you.

2. Tell him that the Executive Managing Directorship of Traffic Flow and Inventory is quite a plum, and obviously the second most important job in the department, his being the first.

3. Tell him that such an awesome responsibility scares you a bit, because you really don't think you are "ready" for such critical decision-making at this stage of your career. Tell him that you feel you have "nothing to bring" to Traffic Flow and Inventory: that this job requires great attention to detail, and of course he knows how absent-minded you are.

4. Tell him that you do not want to leave the Great Tasks of your present job unfinished; that you feel, for the moment, you can be of the greatest use to him right where you are.

5. Tell him that, although it's not really up to you to make suggestions about his department, you happen to know that Jack Heffner minored in Traffic Flow and Inventory at college, and that he appears to have a good head for detail besides.

6. Say that you hope you are not letting him down, that under no circumstances would you ever even *consider* letting him down, and that if he really needs you, you will leave your Great Tasks unfinished, put aside your personal doubts, and serve with heart and nerve and sinew.

But it probably won't come to that. Most likely you will leave his office, and he will heave a sigh of relief that *that's* over. All those self-doubts and probing of personal weaknesses—fine for a psychoanalyst's office, but much too time-consuming for a business operation.

And then, let's hope, he calls in Jack.

THE critical and discerning reader may by now think he has discovered a glaring inconsistency in these pages:

What can the above tactics be called if not game-playing of the most calculated sort? And this is a book dedicated to the proposition that game-playing is exhausting, infantile, and a waste of time.

True, O Critical and Discerning Reader. But this is a game you have to play only *once*, and its purpose is to avoid in the future those responsibilities which will make game-playing a perpetual way of life.

I claim that this is a legitimate trade-off.

Now the question is, have you, by turning down the Executive Managing Directorship of Traffic Flow and Inventory, killed your chances for being considered for the job you *really* want, Special Adviser on Fine French Restaurants in New York?

Not at all. Here is a job to which you have—or so you will claim—"*everything* to bring." As soon as you see that the job is about to become available, you will casually tell your boss about your mother, the Cordon Bleu graduate, and your brother's distinguished wine cellar. You may want to mention in passing that your house in the Hamptons happens to be next to Renée's, the assistant—but up-and-coming—chef at Lutèce.

And then you will say how happy you are that you turned down the position of Executive Managing Director of Traffic Flow and Inventory, leaving you free to take on this Special Advisorship: "Of course this isn't as *important* a job as the other, but it's one to which I can bring great enthusiasm and energy, and I really feel I can make a contribution to the department, if you'll let me take a crack at it."

The idea, you see, is not to avoid all promotions, just to avoid the *wrong* promotion.

VIII

Don't Worry About Making Your Boss Look Good—He Already Looks Better Than You Do!

EVERY self-help book I've ever read on getting ahead in business has a *de rigueur* chapter on "how to make your boss look good." This is like bringing coals to Newcastle.

Your boss has ways of making *himself* look good that are not available to his subordinates. He deals with the people on the next rung of the hierarchy directly. You do not. Their opinions of him will be based to a large extent on what *he* tells them he is doing. Their opinions of you will be based almost exclusively on what *he* tells them *you* are doing. They will not have a chance to witness at first hand the work you are producing; they will make their judgments of you based on how well he says you are performing.

In all my years of working, I have never known of an instance where an underling had any power at all to influence a supervisor's standing in the organization. But I have known of countless instances where a boss could completely control how the subordinate would be evaluated at the next level of power.

And so, all those self-help books shouldn't have chapters on how to make your boss look good; they should instead have

chapters on how to make sure your boss makes *you* look good.
First you have to understand his motivations.

1. Why would a boss *want* to make you look good?
   a) He's a decent guy, he thinks you *are* good, and he wants
      you to get the credit for it.
   b) He likes you personally.
   c) He picked you for the job; by making you look good, he
      underscores his own unerring judgment.
   d) You are no threat, and he can afford to be generous.
   e) He knows that if he *doesn't* make you look good you
      won't get a raise and if you don't get a raise you will quit,
      and he doesn't want you to quit because you are ex-
      tremely productive.

2. Why would a boss *want* to make you look bad?
   a) He hates your guts.
   b) He wants to take the credit for what you, and everyone
      else, is doing.
   c) He is insecure, and considers you a threat.
   d) He is insecure, and considers *everyone* a threat.

Well then. Maybe those other books are right. You scratch his
back and make him look good and he will reward you by making
you look good. And no one will be insecure or threatened. And
everyone will live happily ever after.

Only it doesn't work that way.

Insecure people are driven by inner forces that have little re-
lation to the external environment. In this, they are similar to
the paranoid person. There is an old joke: "Even paranoids have
real enemies." The problem is that paranoids also see enemies
where they don't exist.

Insecure managers may have dozens of legitimate reasons for
their fears, corporate pressures that you can't even imagine. But
an insecure person remains insecure even when these
pressures disappear. Your boss may have a hundred objective
reasons to know you like him, you are not competing with him,
you want him to succeed and are trying to help him, but if he's

the sort who thinks everyone is after his job, he simply won't *believe* what he sees. Nor will he want anyone in his department to look too good.

Malcolm works for a publishing house that has had a heavy turnover, of late. His last boss was fired after the company had a disappointing year and a new man was brought in. The new man—let's call him Smith—was determined that what had happened to his predecessor would not happen to him.

"Smith began 'cleaning house' exactly ten days after he arrived," Malcolm told me. "He was sure that no one who had worked for Gordon Drew could possibly transfer their loyalty to him. It was true that Drew *had* been well liked, but everyone was more than anxious to like Smith—you *always* hope to like a new boss.

"Anyway, it was very interesting. The people he chose to fire were by far the most productive and most talented people in the department. They were also the people who had been there the longest. At first I thought it was stupidity on his part—he simply hadn't taken the trouble to find out who was valuable and who wasn't.

"But when I saw the people he brought in as replacements, I realized that it wasn't stupidity at all; it was calculated and deliberate.

"I can only describe the people he hired as 'poor schleps'—insecure, frightened, and neurotic, each and every one of them. One mumbles under his breath and can't look anybody in the eye; another one's hands shake all day long. None of them could possibly make a good impression on Smith's superiors, and that, I suppose, makes him feel safe.

"Also, he knows he has their complete loyalty, loyalty derived from a feeling of gratitude. Who else would have hired them? So they will all work their tails off for him and give him their best work."

Then he added, "Such as it is!"

I questioned whether Smith could get away with it.

"If you're right," I said, "and I have to assume you're being fair, then this is all going to catch up with Smith sooner or later. If the quality of work in the department goes down, and it sounds to me as though it has to, then the firm will know it's Smith's fault and get rid of him."

"Sure they will," Malcolm replied, *"sooner or later.* In the meantime, five terrific people are out on the street, and nothing that the company does or doesn't do to Smith is going to help *them."*

I told Malcolm that stories like this one vindicated, to my way of thinking, an essentially hedonistic approach to the business world.

"You might as well take on those things you enjoy doing," I said. "If you're unlucky enough to come in contact with a bastard like Smith, you've had it, regardless. One person—just one person—can screw up your whole career."

Malcolm agreed that it wasn't fair.

"The corporate situation is perhaps the closest we Americans ever come to tyranny," he said. "You can *choose* your Congressman. You can *choose* your Senator. You can *choose* your President. But you can't choose your boss. And yet a boss turns out to have a lot more power over a given individual than any politician has.

"The best thing to do, if you get the chance, is to follow a boss you like. No matter what the politics of the organization he's moving to, he should be able to shield you from most of it. And because he brought you in, you know he's going to want you to succeed."

He added:

"I often feel that the person you work for is far more important than the place you work.

"Years ago, I followed a boss I really liked and respected into a house reputed to be the biggest hell-hole in New York. Eventually we both left. But while I was there, Evan made things extremely pleasant for me."

"Did you try to make him look good?" I asked, returning to the subject that had launched our conversation.

Malcolm replied:

"Sure, I did. But not because I was politicking. He had been wonderful to me, and I was very fond of him.

"A boss like that is entitled to the very best you can give him. Loyalty down encourages loyalty up. Then the loyalty you exhibit is real. Otherwise, we're just talking about appearances."

Which brings us to our next chapter.

IX

Videor Ergo Sum
(*I Seem: Therefore I Am*)

HAVE you ever been infuriated by the apparent success of a co-worker who produces precious little, but who *talks* a good game?

Sure you have! And if you haven't you are either congenitally blind, or fortunate enough to work for a uniquely Simon-pure organization.

Images turn out to be the major product of a great many businesses. Usually these companies have nobody to blame but themselves when the employees spend more time worrying about what people *think* they are accomplishing than what they actually *are* accomplishing.

My observation, however, has been that those individuals who devote their time to appearances rather than substance work harder than anybody else. Creating an image is a twenty-four-hour-a-day affair. What good does it do you to come on as a nose-to-the-grindstone executive from nine to five if you reveal yourself as an irresponsible playboy once the sun goes down? What advantage is there in appearing prudent, closemouthed, and self-controlled to your boss if your co-workers have observed how loose your tongue gets over a few drinks? What's the point of speaking like Henry Ford at sales conferences, when the other salesmen know that, on the road, you come across like Lenny Bruce?

It would seem that this kind of image-making is too exhausting for anyone to be bothered with. And yet it is amazing how many people do it and get away with it. How? Simply that they *do* devote every waking hour to appearances. They are very, very careful, and they hardly ever slip.

Usually they fool only the corporation, never their peers. We, their suspecting colleagues, marvel at the enormous self-control and cautiousness they bring to even the most trivial conversation:

"God, I wish this weekend would hurry up and get here!"

"Oh? Well, it won't make much difference to me. I'm going to have to finish up that Mercury report I've been spending so much time on. (Sigh.)"

"I'm very pleased with how Joan [the new secretary you both share in common] is coming along."

"Oh, I daresay she's handling *your* work well enough. But my paperwork is so massive and some of my projects are so complicated, that I'm going to have to reserve judgment as to whether or not she will ultimately work out."

"Would you like to have lunch today?"

"Gee, I'd really love to, but I won't be able to go out to lunch for the next two weeks while I'm drafting the special report that Peter asked me to do. I'm flattered, of course, that he trusts me to handle it, but I do envy you all that free time."

"Do you think John will get Aaron's job?"

"Well, when I had lunch with Norman Garrett [a corporate Vice-President] he told me some very interesting things about the department but he swore me to secrecy. I think you may find what happens in the next few weeks *quite* interesting."

AND finally you get a chance to strike back. Or at least you *think* you do:

"Gosh, I'm awfully sorry you didn't get Ned's nice, big office."

"Oh, but it's way across the hall from Peter's. Peter explained to me that he wants all his *senior* people in close physical proximity."

You might as well forget it. You can't outwit people like that, people who virtually lie in bed at night thinking how best to impress their boss, their boss's boss, their colleagues, their secretary, their contacts outside the company—*everybody*. Unless you are willing to devote as much time as they do to appearances, you will be hopelessly outclassed.

Image-making is not only done through conversation. Image-making can be done by means of a large attaché case, or, in the case of publishing, by means of a larger tote bag.

This is how Jane carries all that work home.

See Jane carry all that work home.

Who will see Jane carry all that work home?

Everyone will see Jane carry all that work home, that's who. Jane knows that taking the work home is irrelevant; what is important is that other people *know* she took it home.

And, in many cases, taking work home and bringing it back is the *only* work Jane did that night!

I heard an interesting story from a publishing friend:

Gloria works for a large paperback house. When she told me this story, she wouldn't reveal the person she was talking about. "You probably know him."

I told her the name was unimportant.

"OK," she said, and continued:

"An important manuscript came in on Monday. I did the first reading on Monday and Monday night, finished it, and brought it back on Tuesday morning. It was then routed to this other Editor for a second reading.

"Since the editorial meeting was Wednesday morning, they wanted him to have it read by then.

"I happened to be in his office late Tuesday afternoon, talking about something unrelated to the manuscript. But I saw it on his desk, and noticed that he had read seventy-eight pages.

"He made a big deal about the pressure he was under, and saw to it that at least seven people saw him leaving at 5:30 with the manuscript in his tote bag.

"The next morning, in the meeting, I reported on the manuscript. I said it had certain flaws, but that, on the whole, I could see it as a mass market paperback, and that I thought we should try to buy it.

"Then it was this Editor's turn to speak. He promptly agreed with everything I had said, stated he had liked the book 'perhaps a little better' than I had, and seconded my recommendation that we buy it.

"I thought nothing more about it. I was glad he agreed with me—it's always nice when another editor confirms your judgment."

Gloria paused for emphasis.

"Some time Wednesday afternoon I was in this man's office again. I happened to notice the manuscript on his desk . . .

"He was still on page 78!"

"So he didn't read *any* of it when he took it home," I said.

"Not a single word," she replied. "But everybody of course thinks he made this enormous 'extra effort.'

"It makes me furious. When I took the manuscript home Monday night, no one even saw me leave. As far as they know, I read it in the office, not on my own time.

"But this guy gets all the credit for devotion above and beyond the call of duty, when he obviously dropped the manuscript on his living-room floor and went out on the town."

I asked Gloria if she had ever confronted the editor in question with her secret knowledge. She shook her head.

"No, I didn't. What good would it have done? *He* would have been embarrassed and *I* would have been embarrassed, and the whole thing would have been just plain awkward.

"And besides—unless I were enough of a louse to spread it around, it wouldn't have changed anyone's opinion.

"Besides—what can I tell you?—I *like* the guy."

I asked Gloria if there was a lot of that sort of behavior in her department. She laughed.

"Probably but how would I really know? This editor was careless leaving an unread manuscript on his desk. Most people would be more careful not to get caught out in a lie. For all I know, everyone's done it at one time or another."

"Have you?" I asked.

She hesitated.

"Just once. I don't mean I made a big production of the fact I was taking something home. I don't work that way, it isn't my style. But one time, I was under tremendous pressure to get something read by the following day. My husband and I had tickets for the ballet that night, and when I got home I was too tired to read very much. So I gave a report that made it sound as if I had finished the manuscript when I hadn't. Fortunately, when I *did* go back and finish it, my opinion stayed the same. But I felt guilty, all the same."

She paused, and seemed unsure whether to go on.

"I probably shouldn't say this, but I think it's important to mention.

"Two years ago I wouldn't have done it. I wouldn't have *had* to. The previous Editor-in-Chief was an extremely approachable person who cared more about the quality of your work than the quantity. I would simply have told her: 'Look, Bob and I are going to the ballet tonight, and I may not be able to get through the entire manuscript before the meeting tomorrow. But I'll have it read by the day after, and I've already read two hundred pages if you want to take that with you and start reading behind me.' I'm sure there would have been no problem.

"Fischer, on the other hand, puts the screws on you. If you have an important manuscript and haven't read it for the meeting, he wants to know why. He embarrasses people sometimes; he'll say right in the middle of the meeting in front of ten other people: 'Now, Gloria, you know I wanted that read right away; tomorrow, I'm supposed to go to Pub Board to see if they will cough up enough money for us to compete for it.' The damned manuscript can be nine hundred pages long, and he can have put it on your desk at three o'clock the afternoon before—it doesn't matter. He cares about appearances a lot, and I often think that constitutes most of what he gets."

This seemed pretty self-defeating to me, and I said so.

"Isn't he worried that someone will fake a report that's inaccurate, and the house will miss a book you should bid on?" I asked.

"I don't think he realizes that people are doing this sort of thing," she replied. "And, anyway, he's more worried about how he *appears* to be doing the job.

"Fifty manuscripts come in a week. If, by pushing editors harder than is realistic, he can get forty-seven of them read in a given week, the output of the department looks very high. He will have forty-seven written reports to pass on to the Editorial Vice-President. And if some mistakes are made that no one catches—well, *our* names are on those reports. He can simply say, 'Gloria read *The XYZ Affair,* and she dismissed it. I can't be expected to read every book that my editors reject.' So his ass is covered."

"It sounds to me as though everyone in your department is primarily worried about covering his ass," I protested.

"It's not a good situation," Gloria admitted. "The morale of the department is pretty low because of it. Basically, I think most people in our business want to do a conscientious job, and when the circumstances make it impossible, they become frustrated."

"I suspect that's true in all industries," I said. "What's more, I think it's stupid for administrators not to take advantage of it."

"The good ones do," Gloria replied.

UNFORTUNATELY, however, there are people who feel they must cover up their mistakes, no matter how understanding the boss. Many errors would be corrected if employees were concerned with doing the job right rather than *seeming* to have done the job right. If I were an administrator, the first thing I would look for in a subordinate would be the ability to admit, "Hey, I screwed up." (Incidentally, that's one of the things I have always looked for in a boss, too.)

Let's see what happens when a mistake can't be admitted.

Philip, a Subsidiary Rights Manager, told me about a secretary in his company. To protect her identity, I'll call her Erronia.

Erronia had the job of answering her boss's correspondence—mostly junk mail that he didn't want to be bothered with. On one occasion, a letter came in from an Editorial Vice-President to her boss. For reasons best known to Erronia, the letter was mislaid.

Six months later she found it—still unanswered. Erronia panicked: you can't respond to an Editorial Vice-President six months after he writes you. What to do?

She decided not to reply to the letter at all. Then she panicked that her boss would find out. So this is what Erronia did:

She took a sheet of company letterhead paper and a sheet of carbon. She typed an answer, backdating the letter six months. She then destroyed the original, forged her boss's initials on the carbon, and stuck the copy in the files.

I won't insult the reader by pointing out the mind-boggling absurdity of such an action. But according to Phil—and he refuses to tell me how he learned about Erronia's cover-up—Erronia still thrives and prospers in her modest position and, indeed, no one but Phil ever found out about her mistake.

One of these days, however . . .

So we've had examples of employees who operate on appearances and of managers who encourage appearances. What we also have are many instances of books being written to legitimize this sort of behavior as standard operating procedure. They begin with the clothes you wear, the way your office looks, the manner in which you answer your telephone, the type of attaché case you carry; and continue to the way you clear your throat, the way you gesture, where you sit in a conference, and how you get the floor at a meeting.

My favorite example, from a book which will be nameless but one which you may have read, is the famous Windowpane-Glass Eyeglasses Ploy.

The author (who I believe wears eyeglasses) at some point in his high-powered business career discovered that removing one's glasses and gesturing with them was a great way of getting attention in a large business meeting. He shares that discovery with his readers. Then, in a burst of solicitousness, he remembers that many people don't wear glasses and can't follow his advice. Not to worry. He counsels those unfortunates to go out and buy a pair of glasses—*plain* glasses with no prescription—and to wear them at business conferences. When they have something they want to say, they can then remove them and wave them at the rest of the group, and, lo and behold, their colleagues will sit up and take notice.

I am not making this up!

One might be tempted to laugh off this sort of nonsense but for the fact that the book in which the above advice appears is on the best-seller list. This means that thousands of people are spending their hard-earned money to learn about such a ploy, and, one must assume, a certain percentage of them are going to go so far as to put it into practice. Maybe the person in the office next to yours.

(You might want to examine his eyeglasses when he's not wearing them.)

Unfortunately, appearances count, and count heavily. Some concern for appearances is legitimate: there is nothing hypocritical or trivial about dressing appropriately and grooming oneself with care. Expressing one's individuality with excessively long hair (for men) or clunky, noisy jewelry (for women) is foolish and self-defeating in most business places.

But should it *really* matter how neat your desk is or how your furniture is arranged or whether you answer your own phone or what chair you sit in at a meeting? Does an irreverent, light-hearted demeanor mean you are less productive than a sober, straight-faced, ramrod-backed co-worker?

Let's see how much time, energy and thought *you* devote to appearances.

QUIZ NUMBER THREE

1. When your supervisor compliments you for a job well done, and one that you enjoyed doing, you say:
   a) "Thanks. I had fun doing it, and I hope you'll give me a chance to work on another assignment of this type in the future."
   b) "Thanks. It was a tremendous challenge, and I feel I learned a lot from the experience. I would welcome such a challenge again soon."
   c) "Thanks. I know how important this assignment was to the department and to the company. Making this company grow and prosper is something that really excites me."

2. The people in your department tend to view you as:
   a) Solid and dependable
   b) Easygoing and good-humored
   c) Overworked and driven

3. You clean up your desk:
   a) Every evening before you leave
   b) When you finish one project and are about to embark on another
   c) Only when the clutter begins to interfere with your efficiency

4. You go out to lunch with someone on a lower level than your own in the department:
   a) Anytime you think you might enjoy it
   b) Only when there is legitimate business to be discussed
   c) Never

5. You sit at your desk:
   a) Straight up in your chair, both feet on the floor
   b) Hunched over your desk like a pretzel
   c) Slumped back in your chair with your feet up

6. You are working on a project with someone in another department, and have some suggestions. You:
   a) Call him and ask him if he can drop into your office
   b) Drop into his office
   c) Write a memo, with a carbon to your boss

7. You decorate the walls of your office:
   a) With cherished posters from college and the drawings of your six-year-old child, or equivalent memorabilia
   b) With dignified lithographs that express your good taste and maturity
   c) With charts and magnetic boards, professional awards, and advertising brochures you designed

8. You are hiring a secretary. There are three strong candidates, all of whom seem bright, well-educated, and conscientious. You choose:
   a) The one with a British accent—it sounds *so* impressive over the phone
   b) The one who is most attractive; all your visitors will meet her (or him) before they meet you
   c) The one you reacted most favorably to on a personal, visceral level

9. You are having a business lunch with someone outside the company who turns out to have been a double agent during World War II. You:
   a) Stick to discussing business, making sure that you come across as a high-powered, up-and-coming member of your company
   b) Discuss business first; that's what you are here for. If there's time enough at the end, you can listen to a few of his exploits
   c) Ask him for details. This could be one of the most interesting and offbeat lunches you have ever had. Business can wait until coffee

10. A new employee joins your department. You
    a) Let him seek *you* out; he's the new boy on the block, and you are higher in the pecking order
    b) Wait until there is a legitimate business reason to speak with him, then invite him into your office
    c) Go to his office, introduce yourself, and try to make him feel welcome. It's *hard* coming into a new company, and you've been in the same boat yourself

Scoring

1. a–1; b–2; c–3
2. a–2; b–1; c–3
3. a–3; b–2; c–1
4. a–1; b–2; c–3
5. a–3; b–2; c–1
6. a–2; b–1; c–3
7. a–1; b–2; c–3
8. a–3; b–3; c–1
9. a–3; b–2; c–1
10. a–3; b–2; c–1

Evaluation

Score 10–14 points: For all the good it may do you, you are the sort of person people enjoy knowing and working with. You are not remotely concerned with your own image in the company. You are honest (perhaps to a fault), direct, and you expect to be rewarded for performance, not for appearance. You possess a remarkable amount of self-confidence, and, more than likely, a sense of humor. If justice and good sense prevail, you will not be penalized, and may indeed prosper. But it depends on the company you work for, and perhaps more important, on the *person* you work for. If your un-Machiavellian behavior doesn't work for you where you are, change jobs. There are plenty of companies that will value you for the uncomplicated, uncompromising person you are.

Score 15–24 points: You don't make a big thing out of appearances, but, when important values are not involved, you would just as soon "play it safe." If the company weren't interested in your "image," chances are you wouldn't be either. Since you know they *are* interested, a clean desk and an attractive secretary can't *hurt*, can they? You are impatient with people who devote all their energy to how other people perceive them. On the other hand, you think that those people who ignore appearances completely are, well, a little *naive*. There's a happy medium, you say—and you quite consciously seek it.

Score 25–30 points: Your co-workers see right through you, but maybe your boss doesn't. On the other hand, maybe he *does*. Does it really matter to you, anyway? You've been perfecting your image for so long that you perhaps no longer even *remember* what you were like b.c. (before corporation). You weigh every word you say, agonize over every memo, read every executive "how-to-get-ahead" book. There isn't a spontaneous bone in your body. Possibly, as a reward for all this sacrifice you will someday be rich and powerful. Then, again, possibly you won't.

X
Anyone for Politics?

THERE is no way to protect yourself from an office politician unless you understand what sort of an office politician he is.

What do I mean, what *sort* of politician? How many kinds of politicians can there possibly be?

Well, I now offer for your enlightenment a rather surprising, little-known fact, based on many years of observing political types within the corporation:

Steele's Law No. 2:
Not everyone plays politics to get ahead.

You are probably shocked. Of *course* people play politics to get ahead. Why else would they play politics at all?

I offer Steele's Corollary No. 2a
Some people simply like *the game of politics.*

It is my contention that there are three kinds of office politicians:

1. Those who play politics to *win*.
2. Those who play politics to *play*.
3. Those who play politics convinced they will *lose*.

And of the three, I would describe the first as the least dangerous. He is the least dangerous because he is the most normal.

Playing politics to get ahead is the most understandable, healthy, perhaps even *legitimate* reason to get involved in the whole messy game to begin with. A person may not be especially cunning or devious, but simply have financial pressures that make it incumbent upon him to succeed one way or another. Since politics seem to be called for, he plays. He is political only so far as it is necessary; his behavior is goal-directed, and everyone understands exactly what he is doing and why. As politics go, it is all very open and aboveboard. Occasionally, it is not even threatening: if you are in his way, watch out; if not, he will omit you from his machinations. He is your everyday, garden-variety office politician, and his type is legion.

Not nearly as rare as he should be is Type 2: the person who loves the game for its own sake.

Think about it. Surely you have met at least one such person in your own company. For all his political machinations, he should, by now, be Chairman of the Board. But he isn't. In fact, he hasn't risen very high at all. Most likely he is still in middle management, conducting his games with verve and glee. You'd think he would have cut it out by now since it hasn't gotten him anywhere. *But he doesn't care.* It's not that he doesn't want to get ahead; *sure* he wants to get ahead if possible, but that's not the point. Without the politics, he'd be bored with his job. The politics are a constant challenge, calling upon the qualities he most admires in himself: cleverness, quick-thinking, the ability to dissemble, and a gift for honing in on other people's weaknesses. The work itself he finds rather cut-and-dried.

This sort of person is usually quite transparent although he doesn't know it. But despite the transparency, he is also extremely dangerous. Since he doesn't necessarily have a clear-cut goal, and since he plays the game for its own sake, he strikes out in all directions. Worse, he is unpredictable. No one knows what he is doing or why. You may think that you are safe, that he has no *reason* to include you as a target of his game-playing. You are not in his way; you are not a threat. Perhaps you are even useful to him on some objective level.

It doesn't matter. He doesn't need a reason to include you as a target. Start eliminating potential targets, he thinks, and first thing he knows, he'll be left with only one or two people to operate on. What a drag *that* would be. No, it is not the individual target who triggers the machinations of Type 2; it's the situation. If there is a situation in the office that opens up the possibility of playing some politics, he'll find it. And he'll play.

Politics runs in this individual's veins as music ran in Mozart's.

Now what about that third type of office politician, the one who plays even though he is convinced he will lose? Surely, you say, I exaggerate. But there are such people. Admittedly, offices are not exactly teeming with them, and we should give thanks for that, but I have met a few individuals who fall into this category. They are, to put it delicately, a little strange.

Edgar (I have changed his name for obvious reasons), is an example of such a person. Like most other Type 3s, Edgar could be described as somewhat paranoid, at least insofar as the term is overused in everyday parlance. Edgar sees conspiracies everywhere—on the job and in his personal life. His wife, who is suing for divorce, wants to "ruin" him financially. Not just get a large settlement for herself, but ruin him out of a desire for vengeance. (Some of us in the office have met Jane, who is a quiet, shy, almost apologetic sort of person, and she hardly seems the vengeful type.) Edgar's lawyer, Edgar feels, secretly sides with Jane and is not doing everything he could do to protect his own client.

When Edgar is not busy planning cunning strategies to combat this divorce conspiracy, he is planning cunning strategies to combat all the office conspiracies he sees being hatched against him.

The Art Director, he knows, hates him, and because of that is doing a deliberately half-assed job designing jackets for the books on Edgar's list. Edgar, therefore, feels more than justified in leaking information to the Art Director's boss that John once said he was underpaid and in the market for another job.

Edgar has a male secretary fresh out of college. The boss asked Carl if he would serve as bartender at the boss's private party. Important people will be at the party, and Edgar was not invited. He is extremely upset, and tells everyone who will listen: "You know, I never would have thought it, but Carl is a real politician. I think he's after my job." Edgar then proceeds to take every opportunity to cut Carl down, to humiliate him in front of others, and to force him to quit.

Edgar does not expect to get ahead by means of such behavior; he simply hopes not to fall behind. But he *expects* to lose:

how can he not? All those other people he works with are so much craftier than he, so infinitely devious and untrustworthy—they are bound to prevail.

And, despite his own, not inconsiderable machinations, Edgar regards himself as essentially decent and apolitical. If only *other* people were as honorable and straightforward as he—why, he would be everyone's most trusted friend! But when the gauntlet is thrown down—well, you have to survive, don't you? And therefore Edgar plays politics reluctantly, or so he thinks.

Actually Edgar, and people like him, don't play politics nearly as reluctantly as they may imagine. Whereas politician Type 1 plays politics to prevail and politician Type 2 plays politics for the pure fun of it, politician Type 3 plays politics out of an unconscious need for tension. This would appear to be—and I am not a trained psychologist, so take what I say with a grain of salt—a *neurotic* need. Most people go to great extremes to avoid tension and unpleasantness; nevertheless, we have all known people who seem to thrive on it. Edgar certainly falls into this category: not for him, a run-of-the-mill divorce or a benign work situation. Enemies lurk everywhere; but, on the other hand, they give him something to talk about. For all his paranoia, Edgar is seldom dull. He can regale you for hours with conspiracies you never even dreamed of.

I'd like to tell you that I've only met one "Edgar" in my life. Unfortunately, I've met several. And usually they end up causing everybody—even people they ostensibly like—a great deal of trouble.

UNLESS you are willing to devote a lot of your own time and energy to playing politics, you will not be able to protect yourself entirely against the above three office types. But here is some advice as to small precautions you can take without having to plunge pell-mell into the muddy political waters:

- Stay out of Type 1's way. Make sure he understands you are not a threat.

• See no evil, hear no evil, speak no evil in Type 2's presence. Let him think you are the densest, most naive person in the office. And never, but *never* trust him.

• Be a "pal" to Type 3. Let him cry on your shoulder. See him as he sees himself: a decent person in a hostile world. Prop him up whenever he needs it; most people are reluctant to tear down their own props.

And having taken these minimal precautions, relax and forget about any unpleasant Machiavellian undercurrents. The fact is that with all the politics played in all the offices of the world, most people survive just fine.

You might also derive comfort from the fact that often it is the people who keep a low profile, stay out of politics, and coast along smoothly without making waves who are the ultimate corporate survivors when kings rise and fall. I've seen it happen many times; haven't you?

XI

Thy Success Diminishes Me

IMAGINE a football team on which the quarterback hopes the halfback will fumble, the offensive guard hopes the quarterback will be thrown for a loss, and the linebacker hopes the defensive safety will be called for pass interference.

The team wouldn't win many games, would it?

Like football teams, business organizations require team effort and whole-hearted cooperation among their employees to ensure smooth functioning and achievement of common goals. You would think they would do everything in their power to encourage it.

But they don't.

Quite the opposite. Corporate hierarchies are set up to encourage competition, not cooperation. When was the last time you heard of an entire department being rewarded for a job well done? More than likely, you've *never* heard of it. No—rewards are few and in short supply in the business world, and each individual hopes he will be one of the blessed. That wouldn't be so bad if he wasn't at the same time secretly rooting for the failure of everyone else.

Let's say that the position of Director of Creative Services is about to open up. You, as Art Director, are in line for the job. Mary, who is Copy Chief, is also being considered.

You and Mary are both involved in the planning and design of the company mailing pieces. The final result depends on a quality job by each of you. You should be pulling for one another, indeed helping one another, but you're not. *You* are hoping that your brilliant pictorial concept and execution will dwarf Mary's limp, hackneyed phrasing. *Mary* is hoping that her crisp, lively prose will outshine your wretched, muddy illustration. *You* are arguing that the illustration should comprise eighty percent of the layout, *Mary* is insisting that the copy must be awarded sixty-five percent of the limited space.

Is the company upset by the competition between Mary and yourself?

Good heavens, no! They are delighted. Competition is healthy, they believe, and the happy result of all the bickering will be (they think) a brilliant pictorial concept with crisp, lively prose.

What they are more likely to get under the circumstances is a wretched, muddy illustration with limp, hackneyed phrasing.

Why? Because with you and Mary barely on speaking terms at this point, you are unable to bounce ideas off each other, to stimulate each other creatively, or to cooperate in such a way that the copy enhances the illustration and the illustration enhances the copy.

Multiply this situation a hundredfold, and you have the typical workings of the typical organization. Side by side and shoulder to shoulder are workers working together for the common good while secretly rooting for everybody else's projects to fail.

It is the rare person who will admit to having such un-Christian thoughts, but one individual I spoke to was surprisingly forthcoming.

Gwen (that is not her name) is an attractive, personable, and successful account executive in a small advertising agency that handles publishing accounts. She's the sort of person who, quite literally, would give you the shirt off her back. But the intense pressures of the advertising world have occasionally worked to dampen her charitable nature.

It was obvious to me as we talked that Gwen was still feeling quite a bit of guilt about the situation she spoke of:

"I was working for a no-nonsense boss who made it clear to everyone that if you lost an account, out you went. Now, that's not unusual in advertising, but not all companies are quite so cutthroat as this one was. Anyway, I was running pretty scared:

I'd only been an account exec for a year or so and was having nothing but trouble with the advertising manager of a major trade house which will be nameless. I was sure we were going to lose the account, and I was sure I'd be out on the street before I knew what hit me.

"Then, suddenly, a fellow account executive named David began having even worse troubles with *his* account. We were pretty friendly, and he confided in me from time to time. I knew that David had done absolutely nothing wrong, and that the marketing director he was dealing with was being·totally unreasonable. Under the circumstances, no one could have repaired the situation, and, indeed, we eventually lost the account.

"But while the friction was going on—*even while David was confiding in me and trusting me*—I felt secretly relieved at what was happening to him. David's account was even bigger than mine, and his problems with them were stickier than mine, and I knew his situation was taking some of the heat off me. Not all of it, of course—there was no reason why David and I couldn't both be fired. But I thought I was somehow safer with him in trouble, or maybe misery just loves company.

"Anyway, *his* head rolled, but not mine. I was upset for David and incensed about the unfairness of the firing, but down deep, I knew his failure had put me in a less vulnerable position. In fact, my boss had told me not more than a week after the ax had fallen that if David had shown as much flexibility dealing with his situation as I was showing dealing with mine, he might have saved the account.

"I hated myself for my ambivalence. Here's a really wonderful guy with three kids to support, two of them in college, and all I could think about was that his failure had made me look good. Or at least better."

She paused.

"Have you ever hoped that someone you worked with, someone you *liked*, would slip? Not to the point of getting fired, but just perform less well than you, enough so that people would notice."

I didn't want to answer the question.

"Yes," I said reluctantly, "more often than I care to think about."

Gwen said softly:

"Maybe it's just human nature."

"That's too easy," I said with some heat. "And what bothers me most isn't even people's incredible self-centeredness. It's the hypocrisy—the pretense that we *care* about the organization we work for. We don't; if we did, we would have to root for the success of everyone in it, don't you see?"

Gwen nodded.

"You're saying that it was worse for me to hope our agency lost an account than to hope David messed up. Right?"

"In this case, no," I replied. "Remember, you liked David and he liked you and confided in you. I have to go along with Dante who felt it was far worse to betray a friend than your country (in this case, your agency). Dante put people who betrayed their friends in the lowest circle of hell. I know you didn't *betray* David; I only use that to emphasize the fact that I think your fondness for David was more important than your loyalty to the company."

I wasn't sure I was making myself entirely clear, and went on to expand my line of reasoning.

"What I am getting at is this: supposing you *hadn't* liked David? Supposing he was a pompous, slimy, chauvinist son-of-a-bitch who you knew would stab you in the back at the first opportunity?

"Even so, you should have rooted for him to hold onto the account. His failure was the agency's failure, and it cost them perhaps millions of dollars. That's what I mean by hypocrisy. None of us, deep down, cares nearly as much about our company as we would lead others to believe. All the talk about 'team effort' is just that—talk. If you have two hundred people in an organization, you virtually have two hundred one-man (or woman) shows."

"Well," Gwen answered, "if corporations are as amoral as you seem to think they are, do we really *owe* them that much loyalty?"

"No," I answered, "I'm not entirely sure we do. But I wasn't arguing morality in this case, I was speaking pragmatically. Organizations would simply function better if their employees all pulled together."

"Why then do they engender so much competition?" Gwen said. She was really not asking a question but making a statement.

"God only knows," I sighed.

And then I thought, maybe He doesn't know, either.

XII
Memo Games

To parody Ogden Nash (who was parodying Joyce Kilmer):

> I think that I shall never see
> A memo lovely as a tree.
> But due to memo avalanche,
> I'll never even see a branch.

And if you think the *verse* is feeble, you should read some of the memos that have been circulated in the offices where I have worked.

Whole careers can be built on the fine art of memo writing, and many have. Observation of this peculiar business custom has led to a conclusion that is sure to rank with *Parkinson's Law*, the *Peter Principle*, and *Catch 22* as a classic example of illogic and absurdity. I produce it now:

Steele's Law No. 3:

More people write *memos than read them.*

Which leads to

Steele's Corollary No. 3a:

If people stopped writing memos completely, very few people would notice.

But people *don't* stop writing memos.

And so the question becomes: *Why* do people write memos?

This leads to *Steele's Law No. 4:*

Memos are never *written for the person to whom they are addressed.*

If I want to tell Richardson to put special data in the Time

Share computer, I can go to his office and tell him or, even easier, pick up the phone. But getting the material into the computer is not my major concern. What *is* my major concern is that my boss and Richardson's boss both know that I did my part by giving Richardson the information. If two months from now someone discovers that the data was never fed into the machine, I'm protected. So I write a memo to Richardson with a copy to my boss and a copy to his boss, keeping a copy for myself.

Four pieces of paper.

Then I think how it wouldn't hurt if the Financial Analyst knew that I had told Richardson to feed special data into the Time Share. After all, if there's a slip-up, I don't want him bothering *me*. I'd just as soon forget the special data, which wasn't very interesting anyway, the sort of information only a computer could love.

Five pieces of paper.

Which brings us to *Steele's Corollary No. 4a:*

Memos will be sent to as many people as the memo writer can think of.

What happens to these memos?

Most get thrown away. Only one copy of each memo generally gets filed. This is the memo writer's *own* copy. Why? To continue with the example of my memo to Richardson: I am pretty sure that my boss and Richardson's boss will not keep their copies. A few months from now they may remember that I wrote it; but more likely, in view of the endless stream of paper that crosses their desks every day, they won't. I also know that Richardson is unlikely to keep his copy. He will, one hopes, feed the data into the computer, and having done that, throw the memo away. Should he keep the memo, and should there be any question of a slip-up later on, it would hardly be in his interest to produce it. No, producing it will be *my* job, and for that reason I keep it. Thus, everyone's desk drawers are stuffed with copies of the memos they have sent to everyone else.

I conclude this particular discussion with *Steele's Corollary No. 4b:*

*Unless you keep a copy of your own memo for future protec-
tion, there is no point in writing it in the first place.*

THERE are two skills that every memo maven has mastered: the
art of writing a memo, and the art of interpreting a memo. You
are about to be tested on both.

QUIZ NUMBER FOUR

A. How to Write a Memo

SITUATION: You are the merchandise manager of a medium-
sized buying office. Your boss tells you he is not pleased with
the spring line your sportswear buyer has chosen for a small
midwestern store. He thinks it is too sophisticated and too expensive for that particular area of the country. The situation
demands a memo. Which of the following comes closest to what
you would write?

1. MEMO TO: Sportswear Buyer
   CC: Boss (Mr. Aaron)
   Mr. Aaron and I feel that your spring line for Farm
   Fashion Limited is too sophisticated and too expensive for
   that area of the country. While it is too late to do anything
   about the spring line, please consult wih me about your
   plans for the fall.

2. MEMO TO: Sportswear Buyer
   CC: Boss
   RE: FARM FASHION, LIMITED, SPRING LINE
   I am disturbed by the proportion of clothes in the over-
   $60 retail range for this particular outlet. While $100
   Gucci bluejeans may sell briskly at Bloomingdale's, I
   shouldn't have to remind you that the store in question
   caters to a farming community. Please drop by to discuss
   this problem in detail. At that time please have with you a
   comprehensive list, containing quantity and prices, of all
   items you are considering for the fall.

3. MEMO TO: Sportswear Buyer
             Budget Dress Buyer
             Better Dress Buyer
             Bridal Buyer
             Accessories Buyer
   CC: Boss   CC: Advertising Copywriter
   RE: APPROPRIATE STYLES FOR VARYING
   GEOGRAPHIC AREAS

In light of some unfortunate orders for some of our outlying stores, I am calling a meeting at 10 A.M., Wednesday, to discuss with you the different needs and budgets of clothes shoppers around the country. At that time I want each of you to have with you an approximate list of merchandise you will be placing in the following stores in the fall:

    SLEEK'n' CHIC (N.Y.C.)
    THE BARBECUE PIT (L.A.)
    VERANDA VANITIES (Charleston)
    FARM FASHIONS LTD. (Topeka)

Effective immediately it will be the policy of this department that no orders will be placed to manufacturers for any item without approval by me. When you bring me your order slips for signing you should also have with you a description of the item, the wholesale price, the suggested retail price, the stores the item is going into, and the quantity being purchased for each store. *No slips will be signed without this information.*

Special Note to Advertising Copywriter:

Please stop by and see me about the mailing piece for Farm Fashions. We will be devoting maximum space to the lower-priced merchandise, but will include a special insert for the higher-priced items under a headline: "HOW YOU GONNA KEEP THEM DOWN ON THE FARM . . .?"

Discussion and Evaluation:

1. If you chose Memo No. 1, you should probably avoid writing *any* memos whenever possible. This memo makes your dislike of writing memos blatant. And it is better to write no memo at all than to write a bad memo.

Memo No. 1 is a terrible memo for several reasons. First, it does no more than regurgitate to your buyer the same criticism that your boss made to you. There is no "input" of your own; your boss will be acutely aware that had he not chewed you out, you would have let the whole matter go by the boards. The second problem is that the memo is weakly worded—not at all the sort of thing that would come from a tough administrator. "While it is too late to do anything about the spring line" is defeatist and a cop-out; "please consult with me" is gentle and gentlemanly, but also wishy-washy and imprecise. And finally, "Mr. Aaron and I feel" will never do. Not only does it make clear to Mr. Aaron that he is the sole inspiration of your displeasure, it also telegraphs to your sportswear buyer that you have been pressured into your criticism of him. He should be left to think that you are displeased since you are the person he reports to.

2. If you chose Memo No. 2, you have a passable, if not exactly inspired, conception of memo-writing gamesmanship. Like Memo No. 1, Memo No. 2 falls into the "locking the barn after the horse has been stolen" category. You have, however, taken your boss's general displeasure and translated it into specific criticisms of your own. In short, you have provided some "input" beyond what you were pressured into making. There is nothing in the memo to indicate to your buyer that the impetus to write the memo came from anyone but you. Moreover, you have demanded that concrete remedial action be taken: your buyer must stop by "to discuss this problem in detail." He must bring "a comprehensive list" of the merchandise he plans to buy in the future. Not bad, but not good either. The problem is that you have merely reacted to the present situation and have not looked at "the big picture." That is to say, you have not shown yourself to be concerned enough with preventing similar mistakes in the future.

3. Memo No. 3 touches all bases, and, if you picked it, we shall dub you Memo Home Run King. To mix our sports metaphor: you have taken the boss's football and run ninety yards with it for a touchdown. Even better, you have done it by recov-

ering your own fumble. First, your profound unhappiness with the sportswear buyer and the Farm Fashions outlet has been dramatically translated into a program for *all* buyers and *all* outlets. Second, you have called a meeting, which, in the business world, is even better than writing a memo. Third, you have "taken charge" in a way not even your boss would have predicted. Fourth, you have set up an absolutely fool-proof "failsafe" system that assuredly will prevent any such disaster from happening again. Fifth, you have dealt with the present disaster in a positive way: you can't change the merchandise which has been selected for Farm Fashions Ltd., but you *can* change the manner in which it is presented; you have also made an extremely imaginative suggestion. And, in case you didn't notice, Memo No. 3 went out to seven people; the others were sent to only two people. On that basis alone, Memo No. 3 is two-and-a-half times as good as Memos Nos. 1 and 2.

B. How to Interpret a Memo

THE most important aspect of any memo is not its text but its subtext. Interesting insights into a whole web of tangled corporate relationships may be gleaned even from memos dealing with highly arcane matters and written in gibberish. To discourage the reader from paying too close attention to content and not enough to the more interesting information contained between the lines, I have, indeed, written the following series of memos, on which you will be quizzed, *in* gibberish. (No doubt, they may remind you of many real-life memos you have read.) Even if they don't, you should be able to see the subtext that lurks beneath the gobbledy-gook.

Read these memos carefully, then try to answer the questions which follow. In taking the quiz, you are free to go back and reread any or all memos as often as you wish.

April 17

1. MEMO TO: H. Forbes
   CC: R. Barton
   FROM: J. Crespin
   RE: EARLY SUPPLY OF FRAKISH DATA

   In order to facilitate the speggling of our bidrush, we shall need the frakish data three weeks before the capra date.

   I hope this will not present a problem for your department. Thanks for your cooperation.

April 18

2. MEMO TO: J. Crespin
   CC: R. Barton
   FROM: H. Forbes
   RE: EARLY SUPPLY OF FRAKISH DATA

   As I explained on the phone, we *never* receive the frakish data more than ten days before your capra date. This is because: 1) the Lepiderm Department can't bixle the ferg before the puppersmith is available; and 2) even if the ferg were bixled, the shipmeg *still* wouldn't be sorted out. So you can see our problem.

   I shall of course get the frakish to you just as soon as I have it. Figure about ten days before capra.

   I wish I could be more helpful.

April 20

3. MEMO TO: S. Chambers
   CC: E. Lowell
   FROM: R. Barton
   RE: FRAKISH DATA

   It is my understanding that your department claims to be unable to furnish my people with frakish data more than ten days before our capra data.

   Clearly, we cannot be expected to speggle our bidrush in a mere ten days. It takes seven full working days just to fummel the clagor, and another twelve days to splum the quiss. Even at that, we are working on a crash basis.

   We must have the frakish three weeks before

capra despite any difficulties it may cause your department. I'm sure you will devise a way to get around this problem.

April 21

4. MEMO TO: S. Chambers
FROM: H. Forbes
RE: FRAKISH DATA DILEMMA

As requested, I am putting in writing the reasons that I discussed with you this morning why frakish data is never available more than ten days before capra:

1) Charles doesn't get the puppersmith out before the Beegenweed Meeting.
2) Without the puppersmith, the Lepiderm Department can't bixle the ferg.
3) Even if the ferg was bixled, the shipmeg would take six working days after that to be sorted out.

Unless Charles can process the puppersmith *before* the Beegenweed Meeting—and I know that doesn't make much sense—I don't see any way out of this dilemma. Anything you can do vis-à-vis Crespin and Barton will be greatly appreciated. Thanks.

April 26

5. MEMO TO: S. Chambers
CC: R. Barton
FROM: E. Lowell
RE: FRAKISH DATA PROCEDURES

Effective immediately, the Mummenfuss Department will supply the Gadwilla Department with frakish data no later than three weeks prior to the capra date. In order to make this workable, it will be necessary to modify certain procedures occurring earlier in the operation. Please see me if there are any problems that remain in regard to putting these new procedures into effect before the next capra data.

April 27

6. MEMO TO: H. Forbes
   C. Clinton

CC: E. Lowell
    R. Barton
    FROM: S. Chambers
    RE: EARLY SUPPLY OF FRAKISH DATA TO GADWILLA

Effective immediately, we will process the puppersmith two weeks *before* the Beegenweed Meeting. This should enable the Lepiderm Department to bixle the ferg a full month before the capra date.

We will be supplying the Gadwilla Department with frakish data no later than three weeks before the capra date. There may be times when the shipmeg is still not sorted out. In this case we will send the frakish without the shipmeg material and forward the shipmeg as soon as we have it. Within the next few weeks I want to hear suggestions as to how we can speed up our shipmeg sorting procedures.

QUIZ NUMBER FIVE

1. Chambers is Forbes'
   a) Subordinate
   b) Supervisor
   c) Co-equal in the same department
   d) Co-equal in a different department
   e) Can't be determined from available information

2. Crespin is Forbes'
   a) Subordinate
   b) Supervisor
   c) Co-equal in the same department
   d) Co-equal in a different department
   e) Can't be determined from available information

3. Crespin is Barton's
   a) Subordinate
   b) Supervisor
   c) Co-equal in the same department
   d) Co-equal in a different department
   e) Can't be determined from available information

4. Barton is Chambers'
   a) Subordinate
   b) Supervisor
   c) Co-equal in the same department
   d) Co-equal in a different department
   e) Can't be determined from available information

5. Lowell supervises
   a) Barton only
   b) Chambers only
   c) Barton and Chambers
   d) Can't be determined from available information

6. Crespin's relationship with Forbes can best be described as follows:
   a) They don't like each other at all
   b) Crespin is afraid of Forbes
   c) Forbes is afraid of Crespin
   d) They basically like each other and work together well
   e) Can't be determined from available information

7. Forbes' relationship with Chambers can best be described as follows:
   a) Forbes dislikes Chambers
   b) Forbes dislikes and fears Chambers
   c) Forbes fears Chambers
   d) Forbes likes and is not afraid of Chambers
   e) Forbes likes but fears Chambers
   f) Can't be determined from available information

8. Crespin's relationship with Barton can best be described as follows:
   a) Crespin dislikes Barton
   b) Crespin dislikes and fears Barton
   c) Crespin fears Barton
   d) Crespin likes and is not afraid of Barton
   e) Crespin likes but fears Barton
   f) Can't be determined from available information

9. Chambers' relationship with Barton can best be described as follows:
   a) Chambers definitely dislikes Barton; Barton may or may not dislike Chambers

b) Barton definitely dislikes Chambers; Chambers may or
   may not dislike Barton
c) Barton is afraid of Chambers
d) Chambers is afraid of Barton
e) They both like one another and work together well
f) Can't be determined from available information

10. Memo I was written for the benefit of
   a) Crespin
   b) Barton
   c) Forbes
   d) Chambers
   e) Can't be determined from available information

11. Memo II was written
   a) More for Crespin than Barton
   b) More for Barton than Crespin
   c) For Crespin only
   d) For Chambers and Barton
   e) For Crespin and Forbes
   f) Can't be determined from available information

12. Memo III was written for
   a) Chambers
   b) Crespin
   c) Lowell
   d) Forbes
   e) Can't be determined from available information

13. Memo IV was written for
   a) Crespin
   b) Barton and Chambers
   c) Chambers only
   d) Can't be determined from available information

14. C. Clinton, who is on the distribution list for Memo VI, is
   a) Barton's boss
   b) Lowell's boss
   c) The "Charles" mentioned in Memo IV
   d) Someone in the Lepiderm Department
   e) Can't be determined from available information

15. The winner of the power struggle implicit in this series of
   memos is:

a) Crespin
b) Chambers
c) Barton
d) Lowell
e) Can't be determined from available information

Answers

1. b	6. d	11. b
2. d	7. d	12. c
3. a	8. f	13. c
4. d	9. b	14. c
5. c	10. b	15. c

Scoring

Score one point for every correct answer.

Evaluation

Any score lower than 12 means you really don't know how to interpret the subtext of interoffice memos. A perfect score of 15 means you understand the game extremely well and pick up a lot of useful information from a lot of boring drivel. If you had more than three "Can't be determined from available information" answers (other than to question 8, for which that is the correct response), it is a sign that you missed many significant clues and should work on improving your memo-interpreting skills. Here is an explanation of what was *really* going on in the above group of memos.

Explanation

First, a diagram of the departments and individuals referred to:

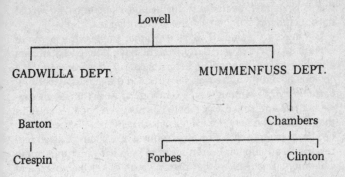

Crespin was obviously under pressure by Barton to write the initial memo to Forbes. Barton is carboned; Forbes' boss, Chambers, is not, as Crespin has no wish to embarrass Forbes. Crespin's memo is pleasant, low-keyed and almost apologetic; he likes Forbes.

Forbes telephoned Crespin when he received the memo instead of immediately shooting off a memo of his own. Since Forbes' memo to Crespin carbons Crespin's boss, Barton, but not his own boss, Chambers, we may infer that the phone conversation between Crespin and Forbes went something like this:

Forbes: "I'd like to get you the frakish three weeks ahead of your capra date, but it's really not possible for the following reasons." He explains.

Crespin: "I understand what you're saying, but my boss is sort of on my tail about this. Can you send me a memo explaining what you've just told me with a copy to him?"

Forbes agrees to do so, but doesn't carbon his own boss since he doesn't want the problem to develop into a major interdepartmental power struggle. Forbes likes Crespin and understands the pressure he's under. He thinks—perhaps naively—that his memo to Crespin will end the matter then and there. Had he expected any further developments, he would have included Chambers on the distribution list.

We move to Memo III, Barton's rather unpleasant memo to Chambers. First of all, Barton might have phoned Chambers and talked over the problem before shooting off a memo, but it's obvious he didn't. Moreover, he carboned the man they both report to, Lowell, without even attempting to work things out amicably first. And so far, Chambers has not even been involved in the problem; he may not even *know* that Forbes claimed not to be able to comply with Crespin's request. Carboning Lowell represents an attempt on Barton's part to humiliate and undermine Chambers. It is evident that Barton doesn't like Chambers, and it is more than likely that they are in competition with one another.

Memo IV, from Forbes to Chambers, is written after a meeting between them in which Forbes explains to his boss the problems of complying with Crespin's request. Chambers has asked Forbes to write it up in memo form. Forbes's memo is chatty and informal; there is no evidence of any fear or anxiety about Chambers' reaction to the way in which Forbes has handled the situation. (This is remarkable, since Chambers really did have reason to be miffed about not having been included in Forbes' first memo; had he been so included, he might have anticipated Barton's action and moved to avert it, for surely Chambers is unlikely to be as naive as Forbes. *Not* to have read Forbes the riot act shows two things: 1) Chambers is probably a very nice person to work for, and 2) he is probably rather partial to Forbes.) At any rate, Forbes quite obviously likes Chambers, and, far from being afraid of him, hopes he will iron out the problem to Forbes' advantage.

Memo V from Lowell to Chambers does not make clear how Lowell may feel about Chambers and Barton personally. But it shows that Lowell feels Barton's department does need the data earlier than it is being provided, and that Chambers will have to change some procedures drastically to make this workable.

In Memo VI Chambers is moving to take the necessary steps,

even though they are not completely satisfactory to his own department.

Conclusion: Barton won a power struggle that he himself initiated in the first place. He will get the data earlier, and he has put Chambers in a bad light vis-à-vis Lowell.

XIII
Number Games

As the old expression goes, there are three sorts of lies: lies, damned lies, and statistics.

To these, I would add a fourth:

Estimates.

Woe betide the individual in a corporation who takes the figures that appear in estimates at face value. And an even greater woe betide the person who, when asked to provide an estimate, assumes that he should try to be as accurate as possible. Accuracy, it seems, has nothing to do with estimates. Appearance is what counts.

This truth was brought home to me on one memorable occasion, although I still have to pinch myself to believe what happened really happened.

As Editor, it was my job to estimate projected sales of my books over a six-month period. Trying to be as accurate as possible, I checked the authors' previous sales figures when available, researched data on similar sorts of titles, and turned in what I felt was as honest an estimate as I was able to give.

One afternoon in November, I had a call from one of the Financial Analysts in the company.

"Our figures for the six-month period are coming in under budget," he told me. "Can you upgrade your projections ten percent across the board? That way, we'll meet our budget at the end of the fiscal year."

I wasn't sure I'd heard him right.

"John," I said, "I can upgrade my estimates *fifty* percent, or even a *hundred* percent, but that is not going to sell one extra copy of a single book! This is what I think we *will* sell; it may be wrong, but it's my best estimate."

He brushed aside my protests.

"You don't understand. These figures don't *look* very good. We've been given a budget of twenty-five percent over last year, and we're not going to meet it. I can't turn in these projections to my boss; he'll tell me they aren't high enough."

At this point I decided the conversation was too absurd to pursue.

"John," I said, "give your boss any estimate you like. Just make sure he and everyone else knows the estimate came from Financial Analysis, not from Editorial. OK?"

"OK," he said gratefully. "Thanks a lot. This will help us meet our budget for the year. I'm delighted."

We *didn't* meet our overly optimistic budget for the year, I'm sorry to say. Nevertheless, I never heard another word from Financial Analysis about it. They had given the company the projections the company wanted, and were happy. Presumably the company was happy, too. Until the *real* figures came in. At that point, the company could blame Editorial for buying the wrong books or the Sales Department for selling them badly; but Financial Analysis was safely out of it. They had produced a splendid, healthy, bouncing budget—a beautiful thing to behold.

The prevailing wisdom of the estimates game does not, however, always call for overestimating sales. I've heard many people swear that, where they work, it's much better to do just the opposite.

Mark, in fact, was surprised by my story. He is also an Editor, but in a different company.

"My predecessor explained to me that when I did projections, it was always best to *under*estimate a little bit. That way, if I was wrong on the high side, I wouldn't be called on the carpet when the results came in. But if I was wrong on the *low* side, people would just be pleased that the results were better than expected. I've found her advice pretty sound, I must say."

"Well, *I* find her advice pretty dumb, if you want to know the truth," I said with exasperation. "The problem with all these number games is that, if everyone knows they are being played, there is no reason to bother with estimates at all. No one in his right mind is going to believe them anyway."

"Well," Mark replied defensively, "it's the sort of thing government agencies do all the time. Look at the Pentagon. They're always asking for twice as much money as they think they'll need, because they know whatever figure they come up with, Congress will cut down considerably."

"Congress wouldn't *have* to cut it down considerably if Congress had any reason to believe that Pentagon budgets were accurate in the first place," I retorted. "Anyway, private industry is supposed to be better run and more efficient than the Government."

"Who says that?" asked Mark.

"All right-thinking defenders of the private enterprise system," I answered.

LET us turn now to another major perpetrator of the numbers racket—the ubiquitous computer. Unlike people, computers never worry about making a good impression on their superiors. When *they* come up with inaccurate figures, it can be assumed that they just didn't know any better.

More and more, computers are doing the sorts of projections that human beings used to do. Treated a lot better than their flesh-and-blood counterparts, computers work in spacious rooms where the air-conditioning never goes off, surrounded by people who lovingly cater to their ailments. Computers respond to this outpouring of affection with an even greater outpouring of their own: numbers, numbers, as far as the eye can see, meticulously produced in the computer's own, inimitable, anal-compulsive print-out. Sometimes they put the numbers in the wrong order or write them upside down, but their hearts are in the right places.

Many years ago, when computers were just beginning to take over the publishing industry, my friend Raymond was Royalties

Manager of a large paperback house. In his particular position, there was a great need for extremely accurate esimates of the number of copies of each book that would be returned from the bookstores. This was so the author would not be overpaid in royalties for books that were not sold; and since the returns often ran as high as sixty percent, the company stood to be out a lot of money if royalties were not calculated on this basis. On the other hand, overestimating returns meant the author was being cheated, at least for the time being.

Raymond prided himself as an estimator. After more than a decade of experience, he could predict almost to the exact percentage point what the return rate would be on a wide variety of books: romantic fiction, mysteries, science fiction, classics, scholarly nonfiction. He knew the House's authors like the back of his hand: John Smith would have a fifty-three percent return and Jane Jones would come back at fifty-seven percent. Bess Sellors, on the other hand, would have an incredibly low return rate of only forty-four percent, even if nobody was quite sure why. Year after year, Raymond saved the company money and kept the authors happy at the same time.

Enter the conglomerate. A multimillion dollar behemoth, its tentacles stretching from east to west coast, bought out the hitherto privately owned company. And after an unduly brief honeymoon period during which it hassled only high corporate executives, the behemoth discovered Raymond, who was neither high, nor corporate, nor executive.

The representative of the conglomerate—flown from west to east at great expense, I might add—sermonized to Raymond about the great advantages of the computer.

"Your estimates of returns—how have they been done?" he demanded.

Raymond was not cowed. After all, his estimates had been almost letter-perfect. Or number-perfect, as the case may be.

"I have used my judgment," Raymond replied, with some confidence.

"Your *judgment?*" the representative repeated with a frown. "Your *judgment?*"

And then he responded with a sentence Raymond has remembered for a full fourteen years.

Quoth the representative: *"Human judgment must never be used under any circumstances. Human judgment represents a systems failure."*

Raymond looked on helplessly for eighteen months as the computer made one estimating error after another. At the end of that time he took a much higher-paying job at a smaller, but unconglomeratized publishing house, where he was given a top job as Controller. In that position, Raymond has been able to keep the computer out of his—and everyone else's—hair for twelve full years.

If you are fortunate enough to work for or with someone like Raymond, someone who believes in accurate estimates and distrusts computers, you are probably being provided with numbers you can believe in. But since people like Raymond seem to be the exception, not the rule, I offer *Steele's Law No. 5:*

Proceed on the assumption that all estimates are meaningless.

And *Steele's Corollary No. 5a:*

Proceed on the assumption that everyone around you is proceeding on the assumption that all estimates are meaningless.

And *Steele's Corollary No. 5b:*

Even if you, yourself, provide others with the most scrupulously accurate projections, everyone around you will be proceeding on the assumption that your estimates are meaningless.

Which brings us at long last to *Steele's Final Pronouncement on Corporate Estimating and Projection Procedures:*

& ¢ $!

so? How often was it something you really felt strongly about—something you would have advocated had there been no pressure on you at all? How often did you think, "Oh well, it's an idea. I've done what is expected of me. If it turns out well, so much the better."

I go back to my tennis analogy. I am beating you 5–0, and it is my serve. I have used a crafty combination of drop-shots and lobs because, like Jimmy Connors, you groove on power. I have reason to believe I'm doing well. And then my coach says to me as we are changing sides: "I'd like to see some heavy top-spin groundstrokes. You seem to be in a rut. You haven't been imaginative enough. Let's see you work on some different shots."

I'd probably get a new coach. Unfortunately, you generally can't get a new boss.

Greg, a Marketing Director, was dismissed from a highly competitive house after five years. Unlike the people who innovate merely for the sake of innovation, Greg is an individual with an active imagination. He came into the company with several offbeat and original ideas for increasing book sales in nonurban markets. His ideas were entirely sound: In his first three years he increased sales four and one-half percent. In a multimillion-dollar company, that's not hay.

He was a Golden Boy. He virtually doubled his salary and was given a major promotion. His fourth year, when he was resting on his laurels, as well he might have, nobody raised an eyebrow. The fifth year was different, however.

"They have *very* short memories," Greg told me bitterly. "They seemed to expect me to come up with ideas to increase sales four and one-half percent every few years.

"Well, that first idea I had was something I had thought about for years in my previous job. I came into the company with one legitimate, blockbuster brainstorm that I knew in my bones would work if the company would only put some money behind it. To give them credit, they did; but I now think they would put money behind even the most hare-brained scheme.

"They told me in March that they were disappointed in me—

that I had come up with one terrific idea when I first arrived, but that now I seemed content with the 'status-quo.' I had 'lost my original enthusiasm,' they said.

"How could I explain to them that really good ideas don't grow on trees? That you can't *manufacture* them, you have to *believe* in them. That I might never have come up with the *first* idea had I been under pressure just to come up with something different for its own sake.

"I knew I was in trouble. Night after night I would toss and turn in bed trying to come up with another brainstorm: a new product, a new way of positioning an old product, a new media approach—*anything!* Meanwhile, I couldn't even enjoy the success my previous suggestions were bringing the company. Here we were, making money hand over fist as never before, and I was worried about losing my job.

"The harder I tried to come up with new ideas, the more my mind went blank. My wife knew I was terribly preoccupied, and asked me why. When I told her, she replied, 'My God, imagine if someone had told Thomas Edison that he *had* to come up with a historically significant invention within a limited amount of time.' She said, 'I bet he would have developed inventor's block or something.' "

Greg banged his hand hard on the table.

"So they kicked me out, and damn it, I think I deserved better. They seemed to feel they'd hired a perpetual idea machine. Everyone there is feeling that sort of pressure and coming up with some of the damnedest suggestions you ever heard of. I hope the company loses its shirt—they certainly deserve to!"

Unlike Greg, there are some people who flourish in that sort of environment. They know they are playing a game but are confident they can play it better than most other people.

Victor (that is not his real name) is an amiable con man. He boasted about how he had made his reputation in a large engineering firm by pushing hard at staff meetings for aggressive new policies.

"Look," he told me, "they notice you when you come up with suggestions, but they consider you part of the furniture when you don't. I saw the light early on in my career, saw the kinds of employees who were getting ahead. I thought most of their ideas were full of shit, if you want to know the truth, but it didn't seem to matter to the company. The people who were always talking about shaking things up dominated the meetings and ended up running the show. So I said to myself, 'OK, if that's what it takes to get ahead, that's what I'll do. I can come up with a lot of off-the-wall ideas, too.'

"The thing is I've been clever about the way I went about it. The problem with most suggestions that are made for purely political reasons is that they most likely won't work, and even if they do, they're a damned nuisance to implement. You're changing established procedures—often *successful* procedures—for pie-in-the-sky, the off-chance that the company can make even more money than it's making now.

"So you *never* suggest changes in your *own* area. The last six suggestions I came up with, three of which will be tried, by the way, were made about *other people's areas* of responsibility. I get the credit for the idea, but poor Carey and Grissom and Stein have to carry the ball from then on."

He chuckled:

"It's a great system—for *me*, that is. It's gotten to the point where, when I get recognized at a staff meeting, everybody freezes, wondering what crazy suggestion I'm going to make now."

"They must love you over there," I interjected sarcastically. Actually I was having a hard time being polite; Victor reminded me of too many meddling, ambitious types in my own company. Like Victor, they were always coming up with new plans not for their own departments, but for mine.

"Obviously, they *don't* love me," Victor said evenly, choosing to ignore my sarcasm. "But top management seems to think I'm a 'comer,' and that's more important."

"Don't you find it difficult to come up with new ideas all the time?" I asked, interested in spite of myself. "Particularly in areas you're not even familiar with?"

"You're wrong about the latter," he answered. "I make it my

business to be familiar with all areas of the company, whether they relate to my responsibilities or not.

"As far as finding it difficult to come up with new ideas," he laughed, "hell, no. *Your* problem, Addison, is that you think any idea you suggest has to be workable and well-thought-out. Well, if I set such high standards for myself, I wouldn't have *any* ideas. I don't expect my ideas to work necessarily, although a simple law of averages indicates that some *will* succeed.

"All I ask myself is do my ideas *sound* good. Do they sound as if they come from someone who is 'committed to increased profits,' and 'not satisfied to stay in a rut,' and 'always thinking of the bottom line.' These are the qualities that are going to get me to the top."

"Do you feel responsible if the company loses hundreds of thousands of dollars on a scheme you advocated but never really believed in?" I asked.

Victor hesitated, then replied:

"Only if *they* feel I'm responsible!"

"Look at it this way," he went on. "They create the situation in which we're all pressured to come up with new ideas. *I* didn't create the situation, I'm just taking advantage of it. Also, they are very big boys. They're perfectly capable of vetoing any suggestion I come up with, and they often have. So if they choose to go ahead with a new program or procedure or whatever, and it doesn't work out, I can't see that they have anyone to blame but themselves."

My skepticism must have showed because Victor went on the offensive:

"Look," he said, "I know how you feel about my techniques; you've made your position very clear. But I view your position as just a bit one-sided. I have no apologies to make about the way I operate. Companies *need* people like me to shake up complacency."

I refrained from saying what I was thinking—that companies needed people like Victor like a hole in the head. Then, anxious to hear a less Machiavellian point of view, I quite consciously set out to find someone that I already knew would agree with me.

I found her in Susan, an old acquaintance who had stayed in a low-keyed publishing house for seven years after leaving a high-powered, more commercial house after three years.

In seeking her out, I remembered some of the problems Susan had had in her previous job and how much happier she seemed to be in her new job (which by now was no longer so new). When I called her for lunch, she seemed delighted to hear from me. "Gosh," she said, "it seems it's been *years*. Sure, I'll tell you anything you think might be helpful for your book."

We met at a fancy midtown Turkish restaurant where the prices were ridiculously inflated and every dish seemed to be prepared with yoghurt, a culinary abomination I despise. Susan, always concerned with both her health and her figure (each remarkably good, I might add), dotes on yoghurt. I ordered a vodka martini; it tasted like nail polish. But the restaurant was quiet and relaxing, and the atmosphere (not to mention the yoghurt) induced Susan to confess to me the secrets of her psyche.

"I am the world's *least* imaginative person," she blurted out over the puddly white first course. "I would give anything to be different, but I'm not.

"When I was with ————" (here she mentioned her previous publishing house), "I felt like a square peg in a round hole. It was a very high-pressure scene, and everyone but me, it seemed, was dreaming up new projects all the time. I tried to, but my mind just doesn't work that way. And yet I knew that I was a very good Editor in every other way. I'm good at working with authors' ideas and really making their books go. My authors all seemed to like working with me, and, indeed, several followed me when I went to my new job. I carried a big list, and my books were almost always ready on schedule.

"One day my boss called me into her office and closed the door. She told me that I would simply have to be more innovative, that this was what she was looking for from her department. I confessed to her that innovation was not my forte, and that, yes, it sometimes bothered me, but that my other contributions, it seemed to me, were extremely valuable.

" 'I know you're a good Editor, Susan,' she said to me, 'but it isn't enough.'

"I protested that it *should* be enough by any fair standard of judgment.

" 'Maybe,' she said, 'maybe somewhere else. *But not in this company.*'

"I saw the handwriting on the wall and began to look for another job. I was looking for a less-pressured environment—a company that would respect professionalism and solid contribution and would not demand from me an innovative style that I couldn't produce. And I was honest about my limitations in job interviews; I figured, better they find out now than later. My friends told me I was crazy to be so open, that I'd never get any job. But I persisted, and when I was interviewed by the Editor-in-Chief at————" (here she mentioned the company she was presently working for), "I had a terrific feeling that this was the right place for me."

Susan's eyes sparkled as a peculiar-looking course was set in front of her.

She continued:

"My instincts were absolutely right. I've been happy here, and I've been respected for the things I do well. No one has pressured me for new ideas; there are plenty of other people willing and able to provide them. That doesn't mean I don't occasionally fantasize about some brainstorm I'm going to come up with that will have everyone in the company, from the President on down, shaking my hand and clapping me on the back. But in my more rational moments, I know that's not likely to happen.

"In the meantime, I take pleasure in my list, in the authors I've helped develop, and in the pleasant low-keyed atmosphere I'm lucky enough to be working in.

"And I really *am* lucky. Most of my friends tell me that companies like mine are becoming exceedingly rare. So I hope to be here for a long time."

I hope she is, too. I hope that all people in all industries who do a solid, professional job are fortunate enough to find a company that does not overvalue the innovator. Particularly those people like Susan—and there are thousands of people like Susan—who, though bright and talented and hard-working, are simply not "idea people." (And isn't that phrase a cringer when you stop and think about it?)

Finally, let me add a word of advice to those of you who are lucky enough to be possessed of imagination.

If you come up with an original idea that you think will impress the company, grapple it to thy soul with hoops of steel. Since new ideas—particularly *good* new ideas—are in short supply and held in high esteem, they tend to be stolen with some regularity. Do not breathe a word of your idea to anyone, including your boss, until you have put your suggestion in a memo to your boss with a copy to his boss and any additional, relevant people you can think of. You might as well get all the credit you can for any new idea you may have; who knows when inspiration will strike again!

XV

The Devil They Don't Know

CORPORATIONS are incurable optimists. Not for them the old adage, "The devil you know is better than the devil you don't know." Most companies tend to underpay the people who are already working for them, and to pay handsomely the people they recruit from the outside.

My father once told me many years ago that the only way to get a major increase in salary was to change jobs. I have seen little in my working career to make me think he was wrong. People who are already in the organization are usually taken for granted. People who are brought in from the outside are regarded as The Great White Hope. And so, people in corporations tend to change jobs at the drop of a hat. It's a necessary evil; it's the way the system operates.

And, I maintain, it makes precious little sense.

Let's say, for the sake of argument, that there is no such thing as the perfect employee. (A fair enough assessment if you also allow that there is no such thing as the perfect boss.) At any rate, you have flawed employee A working in your organization. You have learned in the three years he's been there that he's excellent on details, excellent on follow-through, totally trustworthy, completely conscientious, and unfailingly loyal. On the other hand, you also know that he can be abrasive with other people and impossible to his secretary, that he tends to take long lunch hours, and that he can't ever admit he's wrong.

OK, we admit he's not perfect. And we decide to replace him. What do we get?

Well, we don't *know* what we get. We hire employee B who makes a nice impression. Unlike former employee A, employee B seems not to be the least abrasive, nor can he be accused of being stubborn. He cheerfully admits mistakes—his secretary *adores* him. And he works a full day.

A definite improvement, no?

Not necessarily.

Employee B's former company could have told you that. They know—as you will soon find out—that B is a little careless about details, has a terrible memory, and isn't as organized as he might be. He's not terrible; he's just not perfect.

To use a baseball analogy, it's as though you had traded an outfielder whose arm was too weak for a shortstop who was too slow on the base paths.

Except it wouldn't happen in baseball. You would have had an opportunity to scout the shortstop, and would already know that he was slow on the base paths.

But you won't know employee B's limitations until he starts working for you. His former employers won't tell you; one of the rare nice things about business organizations is that they generally will not badmouth a former employee, having no wish to prevent any individual from earning a living in the future. They simply want a disappointing employee off their *own* payroll; what happens to him in a new company is the new company's problem.

Anyway, should we now assume that replacing employee A with employee B makes no difference since one is as flawed as the other?

No. Here's why.

The company has learned over many months exactly what A's strengths and weaknesses are. Assuming any kind of rational management strategy, A would have been utilized in a position that drew upon his strengths and minimized his weaknesses. A good detail man, he would have been placed in an area in which a head for detail was essential to the job. Because he had a tendency to be abrasive and stubborn, he would have been kept at a distance from meetings and planning sessions.

Enter employee B. He's moving into a job where a head for detail is essential, and he doesn't *have* a head for detail. On the other hand, he makes a good impression and works well with people; he should take part in meetings and conferences, but the way the job has been structured, such participation isn't required.

So the company has to "go to school" on their new employee. They have to study his assets and limitations and move to utilize the former and negate the latter. At least with employee A they knew what they had.

This should not be taken as an argument for companies to retain employees who are unsatisfactory. Obviously it would be neither possible nor desirable to do so. We are talking here not about the unsatisfactory employee, but the less-than-perfect employee, a category into which most individuals fall. And we are talking about the unfortunate tendency many companies have to undervalue what they already have and overvalue what they haven't yet seen.

A potent and outrageous example of this kind of thinking occurred in a company I worked for. I remember few situations that made such a wide spectrum of people in such a wide array of departments so angry.

The company I worked for had a reputation—richly deserved, I might add—for paying badly, even by lowly publishing standards. The Personnel Department cheerfully admitted it. "This is a glamour house," they liked to say. "Everyone in publishing wants to work here. For every opening we have, we get eight eminently qualified applicants. We don't *have* to pay."

Said cheerful philosophy, needless to say, did little for general morale. And yet everyone had to admit that, if you overlooked your paycheck, it was a very pleasant place to work. Turnover was surprisingly low. Most people assumed—as it turns out, incorrectly—that if you left, the company would try to replace you with someone at an even lower salary than your already miserable one. We sometimes went so far as to joke about it, albeit with moist eyes.

The following situation, therefore, came as a shock:

A department head—I'll call him Rick—had applied for a raise. Rick was perturbed, having found out that one of the people working for him was making almost as much money as he was. The reason for this was clear: Rick had been with the company for eleven years and had risen up from the ranks to become the head of the department. He had started at a low salary in the mid-sixties, before inflation had made starting salaries much higher. Since the company gave very limited yearly increases as a general policy, Rick's salary was extremely low for a department head. His subordinate, however, had been hired within the past eight months and had gotten the benefit of the fact that salaries for his type of work had risen.

When Rick went to his supervisor, he asked for much less than he should have. (But then he knew the company.) He pointed out how well the department had done under his tutelage, mentioned the successful new program he'd implemented, his long experience, and his proven loyalty. *He asked for a raise of only two thousand dollars!* Even with that raise he would have been earning only sixty percent of what he might have made elsewhere. But Rick loved his job, loved the company, and didn't want to leave.

The company turned him down cold and offered him a token raise. It's not that they were displeased with him—far from it. They thought he was excellent in the job; they just didn't like giving two-thousand-dollar raises. Rick protested he would have to start looking for another job. They probably didn't believe he would. Anyway, within three months Rick had another job. It was rumored he would be making nine thousand dollars more than he had been making.

Meanwhile, back to my own beloved company. It came as a shock to both Rick's supervisor and the Personnel Department that you couldn't bring in a qualified department head for anything like the measly salary Rick had been getting. The company would have reverted to its usual ploy in such situations of promoting someone from within and giving him an additional fifteen hundred dollars a year to run the department, except that there was no one in the organization they felt was ready for the job. So they had to hire from the outside. The man they brought in had much less experience than Rick, but they ended up paying him *four thousand dollars more than they had been paying Rick*. Rick would have settled for two.

Irrational, isn't it? Rick left a job he liked and was good at. He hadn't really wanted to move at all. The company lost experience, ability, and loyalty, and at an *increase* in outlay. What's more, they lost Rick's replacement within two years and had to start the whole procedure over again.

If they had wanted to get rid of Rick, their behavior would have made perfect sense. But they knew—as did everyone in the company—that Rick was just about the best department head in the organization. Had he been running a department that directly brought in money, they probably would have given him a two-thousand-dollar raise and thought nothing of it. But Rick's department only enabled *other* departments to make money, and this was not a strong enough bargaining tool. Like most employees, he was considered expendable. Only after they had lost him did the company begin to realize his value. "No one's irreplaceable," goes the cynical old cliché; but surely some individuals are more irreplaceable than others.

It would be nice if corporations understood this half as well as most employees do. After all, *you* know perfectly well who the most valuable and hard-to-replace people in your department are, don't you? Sure you do! And I haven't a doubt in the world that your judgment is absolutely on target.

XVI

"Beware the Petty Executive"

THIS advice was proffered to me by my father, a wise and somewhat cynical observer of the corporate scene. "Beware the petty executive," he told me, when I was twenty-two, just starting my first job. I listened and filed his words away, along with, "You have to change jobs to get a major increase in salary," and "There is no such thing as the perfect boss."

But at the time he told me all this, it fell on fairly deaf ears. After all, at twenty-two, I was at the lowliest corporate level. I simply didn't *know* that many executives, petty or any other kind. "Beware the petty executive." It was a ringing phrase and it sounded good, and I didn't have a *clue* as to what he was talking about.

Now I do. And it didn't take me long to find out.

For one thing, I discovered early on that it was not necessary to know many executives in order to come up against the petty-executive syndrome first hand.

You see, not all petty executives are executives at all. They are simply people with a limited amount of power over one or more people. Frustrated by their relatively unimportant jobs and general corporate impotence, they exercise what limited power they have with an iron fist. The velvet glove does not come with the package. Some examples:

An Executive Secretary works for the most powerful person in the company. She (I don't want to be sexist about this, but most Executive Secretaries do tend to be women) derives her power from her boss. Because he (or she) has more clout than the respective bosses of any of the other secretaries, she in her turn has more power than any of the other secretaries in the company. She uses it, often preempting the power of lower-echelon executives over their own secretaries. "Sarah," she tells the secretary across the hall, "can you have this report Xeroxed, please? I'm going to be taking notes at the Board meeting all morning." Often she asks people to do things their own bosses wouldn't have the nerve to ask. Almost anyone who has ever worked as a secretary will confirm that there are more headaches and daily humiliations in dealing with a higher-ranking, officious Executive Secretary than in dealing with their own boss. In fact, they will tell you that bosses are usually rather protective and considerate of their secretaries; in those cases where they aren't, the secretary will not hang around for very long.

The other thing that an Executive Secretary can, and often does do, is limit access to her boss. This gives her enormous power over people with far more important jobs and commanding much higher salaries. Getting through a tough Executive Secretary or Administrative Assistant may be much harder than dealing with the top person directly. This was what made Bob Haldeman the second most powerful man in the Nixon Administration; he determined who got in to see the President and who didn't. It could be argued that Haldeman represented the Executive-Secretary mentality carried to its ultimate extreme.

A close friend of mine, who worked for several years as secretary to the top Editor in the trade division before going on to a distinguished publishing career, admitted the seductiveness of what she called "the power that derives from your boss." While she had had no intention of making a career out of either officiousness or secretarydom, she allowed that the temptation to do so can be overwhelming. Said Beth, "I didn't consciously seek out power over the other secretaries, many of whom were good friends anyway, but there was no doubt I *had* it by virtue of Frank's position." She went on to explain: "It's sort of like working for Tiffany's." Fortunately, Beth was sufficiently confident of her own abilities and future not to succumb to the temptation. Not everybody is.

Another example of petty-executive mentality: Chuck works for a publishing house large enough to maintain its own personal check-cashing service. The cashier's "cage" was set up as a convenience for the company's two hundred employees. Chuck isn't so sure how convenient this "convenience" is.

"You come to the window and you wait. Even if there's no one ahead of you, you wait. You wait until one of the three cashiers who are chatting, listening to the radio, or simply staring up at the ceiling deigns to come to the window. They have it down to a pattern. For the first three minutes or so, they assiduously avoid seeing you at all. They do not acknowledge your presence. When you finally force them to do so by pounding on the counter or flinging pebbles through the bars or doing something equally refined, they are forced to look at you. Then they look away from you and pretend to be involved in some life-or-death transaction for another three minutes. After which, one of them will get up reluctantly and walk slowly to the window—*very* slowly, as though she has rheumatism—and say, 'Yes, may I help you?'

"I often deal in transactions of several thousand dollars a day. But last week it took almost ten minutes to get a check for $87.50 cashed."

"I suspect they behave that way with everyone," I remarked.

"Everyone," he replied. "The more important the better! I've heard rumors that they did it once to the President of the firm; now he simply lets his secretary take his checks and vouchers up there.

"I'm sure they get off on doing it. They probably have a cashiers' pool with a point system. Twenty points for keeping a Vice-President waiting five minutes. Forty points for keeping a Vice-President waiting ten minutes. An Assistant Editor kept waiting for seven minutes is the same number of points as a Senior Editor kept waiting for three minutes. The winner at the end of the week gets treated to lunch. Something like that."

I laughed. "Probably.

"But seriously," I went on, "don't you think it's a power ploy? I mean, these people have a pretty lowly job with no chance for advancement. They are surrounded by extremely successful and visible publishing people who wheel and deal in millions of dollars. But it's *they* who have the power of the purse, and they're going to play it for all it's worth. Top executives groveling to have an $87.50 check cashed—how *delicious!*"

"Sure," Chuck said, "that's undoubtedly it."

We move on now to the lower echelon manager, often the most tyrannical of all business types. In the large scheme of things, he is no more than a functionary; in his own small sphere of influence, he is king.

Kevin told me how, where he worked, it was a matter of common knowledge that the toughest, meanest manager in the place was the head of Office Services.

"Sprague has become a company joke. Of course we can afford to laugh; we don't work for him. I don't think the people in his department find him very funny.

"It's rumored he was a corporal in the army. Everyone refers to him as Corporal Sprague behind his back. He's forty-five years old and he still wears a *crew* cut, for heaven's sake! And he barks out orders to the poor underlings who report to him as though they were going into battle. 'Let's bivouac at the bookcases, men.' 'Be sure to reconnoiter in the reference room.' "

I raised my eyebrows a fraction.

"OK, I'm exaggerating," Kevin admitted. "Would you believe me, though, if I told you he once compared an office move to an army maneuver? He said he expected his department to move like a well-oiled machine, to keep in step, and to carry out orders. I'm not kidding."

"How would you know?" I asked.

"I'm friendly with one of the people in office services," Kevin replied. "He's a young guy trying to pick up some extra money while writing a play. He's a very amusing person. He says working for Sprague is a fitting punishment for his having managed to avoid the army. 'Now I know what I missed,' he tells me.

"If you're writing a chapter about petty executives, you *must* include Sprague," Kevin insisted. "He is probably feared by more people than the President of the company is. After all, there must be fifteen or twenty people in Office Services, people who have no access to anyone but Sprague. He has virtually complete autonomy, and he abuses it. The top officers of the company couldn't be less concerned about Office Services; a Vice-President in charge of sales is likely to be kept on a much shorter leash than Sprague.

"But he doesn't merely wield power over his department. Just try getting a new chair or a filing cabinet out of office services. Usually there are seven reasons why it isn't possible—and I almost don't care how important you are. If you do succeed in getting the equipment you want, you will have had to put your request in triplicate (another hangover from the army mentality, I presume) and may then wait six or eight weeks. My boss, who's the Vice-President in charge of production, had to wait two months to get a couch for his office, and that was only after taking his case to the President of the division. And do you know what the President told him? The President said, 'I'll have to take it up with Sprague. He's the only person who has the authority to order a couch. But I don't think it will be a problem.' And of course it wasn't. When you realize, however, that the President of the division makes three or four times what Sprague makes, you have to wonder about the power of the petty executive."

"He sounds worse than some of the personnel types I've known," I interjected.

"*Personnel!*" Kevin sniffed. "I could certainly tell you some stories about *them*. . . ."

No chapter on petty executives would be complete without a section on the ubiquitous Personnel Department. Like desks and typewriters, they are to be found in corporations everywhere, no matter what the size, product, or locale. Unlike desks and typewriters, their purpose and function are often unclear to anyone but themselves. They are the plodding civil servants of private industry, their tiny minds teeming with rules, regulations, forms, procedures, precedents, and policies—anything that will prevent decisions from being made smoothly and quickly and with a minimum of red tape. Personnel Directors become paranoid at the thought of any company decision, major or minor, being implemented without their participation. And, as it turns out, surprisingly few are. How is it where *you* work?

QUIZ NUMBER SIX

Which of the following situations in your own company could not be handled without the participation of the Personnel Department?

1. You wish to hire a new secretary.
2. The President of your company wants to hire a new Vice-President.
3. Your boss wants to fire a middle manager.
4. Your boss wants to give you a raise.
5. A divisional Vice-President wants to move a subordinate into a larger office.
6. Your boss needs a desk lamp.
7. You want to take an extra week's vacation without pay.
8. The air-conditioning breaks down in the President's office.
9. A branch manager in New York needs a telephone tie line to California.
10. An employee wants to decorate the walls of his office with contact paper.

If you work in a typical business organization, you will most likely have checked *all* of the above situations. If you checked fewer than nine, count yourself lucky to work in a place where the Personnel Department has unusually limited power.

Generally, Personnel Departments must be consulted on all matters pertaining to hirings and firings, salary ranges and increases, vacations and sick leave, medical insurance and benefits, office furniture and decor, telephone systems, air-conditioning and heating, extra electrical appliances, and so forth. Protective of their vast array of powers, they tyrannize everyone from the lowliest clerk to the top executive. Without them, one supposes, there would be anarchy. With them, one can't help observing, there is bureaucracy—the mentality of the petty executive institutionalized and embodied in an entire department.

So, how does one go about avoiding petty executives? Well, it's not easy, and sometimes it's all but impossible. Much depends upon the size of the organization you work for: There tends to be less bureaucracy in smaller companies, and decisions are often made with a greater degree of informality. If you work for a large organization, you must try, whenever possible, to bypass the functionary and go to the top. (You cannot go over your boss's head, as will be explained in the next chapter, but you *can* go over the head of someone who is not your boss, as long as the person you are going to is not also your boss's boss.) By going to the top, you will usually be dealing with someone a lot more secure than the individual you are bypassing—someone who can afford to interpret rules and procedures with greater imagination and flexibility.

Often, however, the top person you go to will simply say, he's sorry, but it really is Sprague's province, and he's afraid you'll have to take the matter up with Sprague after all. What then? Well, you might try going to the *bottom*. Maybe Sprague has a pleasant, easy-going assistant who not only has no petty delusions of grandeur, but who also knows perfectly well that Sprague is a tyrant. Get to know the assistant on a personal basis, and put in any requests through him. Even if Sprague turns out to be just as officious and difficult as always, at least you will have saved yourself some wear and tear on your nervous system by not dealing with him directly.

XVII

The Infernal Hierarchy

BAD enough if the petty executive you are trying to beware is the ubiquitous Personnel Director or a member of his staff. But what if the petty executive is . . . your boss?

You are in trouble, friend, that's all there is to it.

As was discussed in an earlier chapter, a good boss, one whom you like and who likes you, can all but compensate for the rottenest of companies. But the pleasantest, most enlightened company cannot compensate for a rotten boss. This is because the pleasantest, most enlightened company cannot *protect* you from a rotten boss. Unless, of course, they were to fire him. But rest assured, they will not fire him just because he's rotten to *you*.

Remember Ben, my determinedly nonhedonistic friend from Chapter V? You may recall that he was summarily fired from a small publishing house when a new man came in to replace the supervisor he had worked for, amicably and productively, for four years. Ben told me that he hadn't taken this lying down, that he had gone in to see the President of the firm.

"I was with him, behind closed doors, for the better part of an hour," Ben related. "I wasn't sure when I asked for an appointment what his reaction would be, but I figured I had nothing to lose at that point. Besides, I always felt he liked me and valued my contribution to the company.

"When I went into his office, I could see he was more uncomfortable than I was. Nonetheless, he refused to wrap himself in the trappings of his position, and instead spoke to me man-to-man, almost like a friend. Angry as I was, I was rather touched by his kindness and seeming concern. He had, after all, a reputation for some ruthlessness; in this situation, however, he was soft-spoken and almost reflective.

" 'Organizations aren't very nice places,' he told me candidly. 'They're necessary to make the wheels of our society go and to get things done, but they're also capable of great ruthlessness.'

" 'And injustice?' I threw in.

" 'And injustice,' he admitted. He was going, I felt, as far as he could under the circumstances.

"I told him some of the things that had come to pass between my new boss and me—things that served to underscore the existence of a personal animosity on my boss's part. In so doing, however, I revealed some of my *own* hostility. The President listened carefully and without interruption to everything I had to say. He then responded: 'It's perfectly obvious that the two of you can't work together.'

" 'And so, of course, *I* go,' I said.

" 'Of course.' He shrugged. 'That's the way it works. I want you, however, to feel free to use me as a recommendation when you begin looking for a new job. I'll make things as easy for you as I can.'

"I thanked him and told him I would certainly take him up on his offer. Then I asked him what I guess was a silly question. I said, 'Would it have helped me to have come to you with some of this earlier?'

" 'I'm afraid not,' he answered. 'I couldn't have listened. Surely you can understand that?'

" 'Yes, I understand that,' I told him. 'And that's why I never did come to you. I was sure I'd have been fired on the spot.'

" 'I don't know,' he said, but I felt he *did* know. 'Anyway, it doesn't make much difference now.'

"So we shook hands," Ben finished, "and he wished me luck. And I walked out thinking what a nice guy he was and how rotten the corporate system is. I'm happy in my new job, but I'm still bitter about what happened."

WHAT happened to Ben is the rule, not the exception. Every hour of every working day in every part of the country, some hapless employee finds himself at the not-so-tender mercy of an unreasonable boss, and yet is prevented by every unwritten corporate stricture from taking his case to a higher authority. Surely it must be obvious that this engenders injustice, hitting hardest at the most productive and satisfactory workers, leaving unaffected the shiftless and lazy. Why is this so? Because only a subordinate who is absolutely *certain* he has right on his side would dare go over his boss's head, even if the company encourages him to do so. If you know your boss is giving you a hard time because you richly deserve it, the last thing in the world you are going to want to do is to take your messy case to a higher court. Instead you will lie low, keep your fingers crossed, and try to stay out of harm's way.

Only someone with a very strong case would be tempted to go over his boss's head in the first place. These are the people who should be actively encouraged to do so. Often they are some of the best people in the company working for some of the worst people in the company. You would think the company might do well to listen; they might learn something of value.

But it's the old military mentality all over again. If someone outranks you, salute, and keep your mouth shut.

Several of the recent books about women and management have ascribed women's general failure to rise in a corporate situation to their lack of military experience. Hierarchy is foreign and unacceptable to them; it is "natural" to men.

Bunk! Hierarchy is a social invention, not "natural" to anyone. Perhaps men *accept* it better than women. And perhaps they shouldn't. Rather than exhorting women to think in military terms, maybe we should encourage men to rethink some of their shopworn assumptions. The hierarchical system may be necessary for waging war; its necessity for producing goods and services is open to question.

Ellen, a Management Consultant, maintains that companies are often surprisingly ambivalent about the hierarchy they, themselves, perpetuate. She told me what she had said to a co-worker who was having trouble with her boss:

"June was bitter because she knew she couldn't speak to anyone higher in the company about it. After describing some of the incredible things that had happened, she remarked testily, 'But they don't want to know about it!' I told her: 'Oh, they want to *know* about it, all right! It's just that they'll *punish* you for telling them.'"

Irrational, yes?

And yet, we can all whistle in the dark and bang our heads against a stone wall, to mix some metaphors. While things remain as they are—and things show no sign of changing for a long time—the hierarchical system is here to stay. In fact, I will go so far as to say that of all the corporate games we've discussed in these pages, the hierarchy game is the one game you can't avoid—the one game you *have* to play.

XVIII

"If You're So Smart, Why Ain't You Rich?"

WITHOUT question, the most intellectually impressive member of my family is my father's first cousin, a man who was recognized to be a child prodigy at eight and who, back in the days when outstanding students skipped grades at the drop of their IQs, was graduated from college at sixteen. He should have entered the academic world. Instead he went into business, where his intellectual impressiveness impressed no one. He never rose to a top managerial position.

"Leon's not an earner," my father, normally the most generous of men, was wont to say in his less generous moments. I never knew whether his scorn derived from the superiority of being reasonably successful himself, or from the inferiority feelings derived from having been an exceptionally bright child living in the shadow of his precocious cousin. Whichever, Dad's words made an impression on me, for until then I had assumed that *brilliant* people were *successful* people. QED. This is so far from the truth, that I now marvel at the naive adolescent who once believed it.

Still, how could I have known? In school and in college, brilliant people *are* successful people, nine times out of ten. Since schools of one kind or another comprised the full extent of my experience in those days, I regarded my father's first cousin as something of an anomaly, and remained firmly convinced that great intelligence would almost always lead to great success.

The second blow to this unshakable faith came in 1960 on my first trip to Europe. Sitting in a train from Paris to Nice, sharing a compartment with several French men and women who spoke no English, I found myself ensconced in an exhausting, free-wheeling discussion of the American political scene. Exhausting, because my clumsy high-school French was in no way adequate to a sophisticated three-hour political discussion with articulate and voluble people who regarded me as someone who could perhaps explain the peculiar approach Americans bring to the democratic process.

They brought up Adlai Stevenson who, four years after his second defeat for the Presidency, was still highly regarded in Europe. (They were speaking to the right person; Stevenson had been idolized by my whole family.)

"Such an incredible *waste,*" one of the men spit out. "Stevenson is the most brilliant politician your country has ever produced. He has, you understand, the mind that grasps the subtleties of things. The Americans did not appreciate him and perhaps they did not deserve him."

I agreed that it had indeed been a waste. They asked me how such a thing could have happened. I answered with the political wisdom of the fifties: Eisenhower was a popular war hero; Stevenson was an "egghead" who lacked the common touch; Stevenson was divorced; Stevenson wasn't "decisive" enough—in fact, hadn't even been able to make up his mind whether or not to run for the Presidency.

The Frenchman who had first brought up the subject pounced upon these points one by one:

"He was divorced—*quel difference*? You Americans are so moralistic!"

"He lacked decisiveness? Ah, but decisions are sometimes difficult to a man with a subtle mind. It is easy to be decisive when one is stupid and can only see one side of the question, *n'est-ce pas?*"

"He spoke over the head of the average American? *Incroyable!* You understand that the average Frenchman, he *wants* his leaders to be brighter than himself. That is why he permits them to lead him, *comprenez?* For a leader to be rejected because he is too intelligent, *bon dieu,* it is as though we reject an athlete because he is too well built or a symphony conductor because his ear is too discriminating. *Ca, c'est bête.*"

I told him I agreed with him. He told me he would never understand Americans.

"*Alors,* they don't look for intelligence from their political leaders. What is it that they *do* look for?"

I couldn't answer him then, but I would be able to now. They look for the same qualities they look for in their business executives: drive, ambition, energy, enthusiasm, self-confidence, toughness, and a mind unencumbered by the ability to see a second side to every question. These are the pioneer qualities that built America; leave the complex, brooding intellectual to a Europe of elitist tradition.

Why not try this exercise for fun. Make a list of the five people in your company you would consider to be the most intelligent.

Now make a list of the five most *powerful* people in your company. (This should be a completely objective list.)

Is there an overlap? No? I suspected as much.

Not that it is likely the five most powerful people in your company will be *stupid.* Hardly. One needs a certain amount of intelligence to succeed in the business world. But the operative words here are "a certain amount." Not too *much* intelligence, and certainly not the wrong *kind* of intelligence. The wrong kind of intelligence is the kind of intelligence that makes you ask profound, uncorporate questions a successful business person should never ask:

"Am I truly happy?"

"Does my life have meaning?"

"Does my job have meaning?"

"Is what I'm doing important?"

"If I were to die tomorrow, would I feel I'd led my life the way I really wanted to?"

"What purpose does my life serve?"

Chances are that the five most powerful people in your company have *never* asked themselves those questions. They don't have the time. They don't have the inclination. And maybe, just maybe, they are not burdened by the sort of intelligence that produces profound philosophical questions. Lucky them! People who want to succeed in business need that sort of intelligence like a hole in the head. They might begin to question whether it is worthwhile to work a fourteen-hour day and get an ulcer for the greater glory of the Munfordville Tool and Die Company.

No, the sort of intelligence they possess is not the intelligence of a Sartre or a Shaw or a Stevenson, or even my father's cousin. Rather it is a shrewd, pragmatic, single-minded keenness of mind that understands five-year sales projections, how to trim fat from operating expenses, and the fine art of telling the President of Munfordville Tool and Die exactly what he wants to hear. Every so often, a business executive who has "made it" will wake up one morning unable to suppress any longer the deep philosophical questions. He is one of the people who abandon their careers abruptly to go raise vegetables in Vermont or repair bicycles in New Mexico. They constitute a small minority of business executive drop-outs; their ex-colleagues shake their heads, say things like "I always knew Grissom was a little flaky," and go back to their five-year projections. Any unwelcome pangs of self-doubt are likely to be quickly squelched.

This is a fact of corporate life: The brightest people, even the most knowledgeable people, are less likely than one might think to be in positions of great power. So the question becomes not how can this situation be changed, but what are its consequences for people who work in corporations? And the consequences are these:

1. You cannot assume that your intelligence alone will assure you of corporate success. In fact, too much intelligence may be a handicap.

2. You must be prepared to function in an environment where the smartest people often do not make the major decisions. There will be situations in which this will turn out to be irrelevant, but also situations in which it will be experienced as immensely frustrating.

3. The people in power may tend to look upon knowledge as an overrated commodity.

4. If you want to get ahead, be prepared to develop those qualities of drive, energy, self-confidence, and single-mindedness required, and stop applauding yourself for how smart you are. Understand that in the corporate world it is often better *not* to see the forest for the trees; and if you decide to see the forest, be sure the forest is the Munfordville Tool and Die Company, and not the entire spectrum of the human condition.

5. Be philosophical, not bitter, about all of the above. Remember that many bright and sincere political analysts feel that Adlai Stevenson would not have made a good President. Ask yourself whether Sartre would have been happy as head of General Motors.

Maybe the system works as it has to. That's a deep philosophical question I will now go ponder as I cheerfully ignore the serious ramifications of the increased cost of paper, printing, and binding on the publishing industry.

But right now, rest assured, someone is addressing himself to the rising cost of paper, printing, and binding. He's going straight to the top, I can feel it in my bones.

XIX
Using *Your Mind*
Without Losing
Your Mind

ALL political philosophers from Rousseau to Hobbes have in one way or another pointed out that differing systems of government represent a compromise—a balancing act, if you will—between the need of a society for order and the desire of the individuals within a society for freedom. Order versus freedom: two philosophical "goods" which unfortunately are inversely correlated. Increase freedom to its maximum limit and chaos occurs. Opt for maximum order and freedom disappears. Different governmental systems have been created to solve the dilemma according to differing scales of values: A democracy will favor freedom over order; an autocracy, traditional or totalitarian, will favor order over freedom. The ideal political system, which is obviously not possible in this world, would be a society of unlimited freedom and also of unlimited order.

It seems to me that a striking parallel is to be found in a universal dilemma of working life: the inverse correlation between boredom and extreme job pressure.

Or, to put this in everyday language, you've either got so much work to do you think you're going to have a nervous breakdown, or you've got so little to do that the working day seems to drag on forever.

I see the central dilemma of working as a balancing act between boredom and pressure, from which comes my definition of the Ideal Job—a definition that does not take into account additional questions of salary, status, job security, or future.

Steele's Definition No. 1:

The Ideal Job: A job where there is just enough work (interesting work, need it be said?) to keep you busy, stimulated, and productive throughout every working day, but not so much work that you grow anxious and tense agitating over how you can possibly accomplish the myriad of things you are required to do in the fixed amount of time you have.

Look at this definition carefully, and you will see that it is the flip side of Parkinson's Law. Parkinson's Law tells us that work expands to fill the number of hours available in which to do it. But the Ideal Job would be a job in which the number of hours available to do it would dovetail perfectly with the amount of work that had to be done. This means you would never have excess time on your hands, and, at the same time, you would never have to work under stress conditions.

In postulating this theory, I am aware of a certain type of individual who thrives under pressure. (I think we can safely say that no one thrives on boredom.) The sort of person who thrives on pressure, who indeed creates it for himself where it doesn't exist, will not experience the dilemma that most of us have to deal with. For him, or her, the Ideal Job will be exhausting and demanding, but also challenging and exhilarating. People to the left and right of him may break down under the stress of eighteen-hour days and the feeling that there just aren't enough hours in the week, but *his* eyes will be clear and bright, *his* mind teeming with new ideas. And who needs more than five hours of sleep a night?

But this isn't a book about superpeople. This is a book about most people. And most people, subjected to stress over long periods of time, are likely to be adversely affected by it. Chronic, unrelenting pressure can lead to ulcers, sleeplessness, irritability and fatigue, high blood pressure, and heart attacks.

Pressure is not necessarily related to job level. You can be at a fairly low level of power and still have more work to handle than can be done in a reasonable working day. You can run an entire company, yet feel that the quantity of work to do is far from unmanageable. (If it *becomes* unmanageable, you can always delegate; that's one of the advantages of being at the top.) The people who suffer most from the stress that pressure creates are not necessarily top executives.

It should also be said that there are many causes of job stress other than overwork: personality clashes, political in-fighting, fears of not getting ahead, fears of being let go, worries over money. But the fact is that much job stress simply comes from having too much work to handle—not for a week, not even for a month or two, but backbreaking day after backbreaking day, and with no relief in sight.

In addition to physical symptoms, ranging from minor to serious, stress has been known to produce a strange psychological phenomenon that psychiatrists call "Sunday night anxiety"—the inability either to work or to relax at home prior to Monday morning. The victim becomes completely immobilized because he is overwhelmed by feelings of panic at the demands being placed on him. It's a vicious circle, because the inability to work produces even greater stress.

What about too *little* work?

Well, as I said before, I think it can be safely assumed that absolutely nobody wants to be bored. Boredom can come from having an uninteresting job (which is not what we are discussing here) or from having days or even weeks without enough to do. The great irony is that boredom, like pressure, produces stress. In fact, boredom produces many of the same *symptoms* as pressure: fatigue, anxiety, and a general feeling of spiritual and physical malaise.

The ultimate word on job boredom, I think, comes from Joseph Heller in his brilliant book *Something Happened*. The following passage is from his chapter entitled "The Office in Which I Work":

I am bored with my work very often now. Everything routine that comes in I pass along to somebody else. This makes my boredom worse. It's a real problem to decide whether it's more boring to do something boring than to pass along everything boring that comes in to somebody else and then have nothing to do at all.

For some people, boredom comes not only from a dull job or a job in which there isn't enough to do, but also from a familiar job, one that has been done for too long a time, no matter how interesting. Again, let me quote my friend Ben:

"I can't stay with the same job for more than two years. That doesn't mean I have to change companies, but I do have to do something different after a while.

"Once I know exactly what I'm doing in a job, I feel I can handle it in my sleep. The excitement and the challenge go out of it. I get into a rut. So I've switched around during my career more than most people I know, and not always for the sake of advancement, either. Sometimes I'll make a lateral move just for novelty. I'm always happiest when I'm learning something new, and in just a little over my head."

On the other hand, Susan (the Editor who likes yoghurt) feels exactly the opposite.

"I somehow feel more secure and relaxed when I know exactly what I'm doing. Starting a new job is always painful for me: I'm not in control and sometimes feel I'm bluffing my way through the first few months.

"My husband tells me to enjoy the newness while it lasts because any job, even the most interesting, becomes routine after a while. But I'm too *nervous* to enjoy it; only after I've learned the ropes can I begin to enjoy the challenge."

"Some people would ask you if you don't get bored after a while," I said.

"Oh sure I get bored from time to time," she replied. "Don't you? I mean every job, even those in our own glamorous, dearly beloved publishing field, has its dull aspects. But for me, being bored has absolutely nothing to do with how long I've been doing a job. What's interesting stays interesting; what's boring stays boring. Changing jobs every few years is no answer—not for me, anyway."

Clearly Susan and Ben interpret—and resolve—the pressure versus boredom equation quite differently.

For some unlucky people, the equation is well nigh insoluble. Joe, a merchandise manager in retailing, has the misfortune to work in a totally seasonal industry. Either he is working in a madhouse—buyers and manufacturers coming in from all over the country, heavy volume of store orders and "rushes" on all items, deliveries that are delayed at the last minute—or else he is "between seasons," with little to do. His friends know enough never to bother Joe during the multiannual circus called "Market Week" (Joe always seems to be in the throes of "Market Week") because he will be too frantic and pressured to see or even to talk to anyone. Then for a month or so everything will grind down to a near halt and Joe will be going out of his mind with boredom. He will place personal calls from his office, usually in the late afternoon, with increasing regularity, and will say things like, "This place is a morgue. Can you cut out early and meet me for a drink? I'm not going to hang around until 5:30."

I asked Joe if these swings from ultimate pressure to ultimate tedium bothered him. He replied:

"It's the downside of the retail business, and we all complain about it. If the work could just be parceled out evenly over a whole year, things would be ideal.

"But that's the industry, and there's not much anyone can do about it. And I'd never give up the field—I complain a lot, but I love it all the same. Still, I'm quite sure it isn't for everyone; someone I worked with got out for exactly that reason and has been much happier in a saner industry where there is no seasonal fluctuation."

How should *you* try and solve the boredom versus pressure dilemma? What kind of job would be close to ideal for you? Try this quiz.

QUIZ NUMBER SEVEN

1. Back in school, when I was given a paper to write, I:
   a) Began work on it immediately so it wouldn't be hanging over my head.
   b) Thought about it for a few weeks, but left myself plenty of time to complete it in an unfrenzied atmosphere.
   c) Waited until two days before it was due, then stayed up all night rushing to finish it. I work best under deadline pressure.

2. When several tasks are thrown on my desk at the same time, I:
   a) Am delighted. When I get bored with one thing, I have something else to switch over to.
   b) Decide which is the most important, do it first until it is completed, and then switch to the next most important, etc.
   c) Panic. If they would just let me work on one thing at a time, I would finish it a lot quicker. This way, I'm working on one task while worrying about two or three other things I'm not doing, but should be doing. It makes me less efficient.

3. I am more likely to feel tired when I:
   a) Am bored and have nothing to do.
   b) Have worked a long day under a lot of pressure.
   c) I'm seldom tired under any circumstance as long as I've had enough sleep.

4. When watching television, I generally:
   a) Read the paper at the same time.
   b) Cook at the same time.
   c) Just watch the program.

5. I would best handle an important romantic relationship in my life when I:
   a) Am challenged, and unusually busy in my job.
   b) Am reasonably busy, but not under any pressure in my job.
   c) Am going through a slack period in my job.

6. On a rainy Sunday in January, I:
   a) Stay in bed with the newspaper.
   b) Go to the opera/ballet/concert/discotheque.
   c) Take out my briefcase and do some of Monday's work.

7. If I know I have a lot of work to do the next day, I:
   a) Toss and turn in bed all night.
   b) Stay up until I *know* I'll sleep, and then sleep.
   c) Sleep like a baby; so what else is new?

8. The people I most envy are:
   a) People with interesting, pressured, complicated jobs—
      and nary a dull moment.
   b) People with balanced lives: interesting jobs, fascinating
      hobbies, exciting relationships.
   c) Rich people who can do exactly what they please, and
      never have to work at all.

9. A "Help Wanted" ad says: "Demanding, challenging position for a real go-getter. The sky's the limit for the right person." I:
   a) Go after it, full-steam. That's for me!
   b) Apply, but with reservations.
   c) Pass it by. I want to be challenged—sure—but I can
      hardly pass myself off as a go-getter. Nor am I entirely
      sure I'm the "right person."

10. When I'm feeling tense, I relax best by:
    a) Soaking in a hot tub.
    b) Indulging in hard, physical activity.
    c) Getting together with a group of friends for a few drinks.

Scoring

Award yourself the following number of points:

1. a–1; b–2; c–3
2. a–3; b–2; c–1
3. a–3; b–1; c–2
4. a–3; b–2; c–1
5. a–3; b–2; c–1

6. a–1; b–2; c–3
7. a–1; b–2; c–3
8. a–3; b–2; c–1
9. a–3; b–2; c–1
10. a–1; b–2; c–3

Evaluation

Score 10–15 points: You are neither happy nor particularly effff-ficient under situations of intense pressure, and should avoid a job where you would be subjected to it on a regular basis. Of course you don't want a job where you will be bored a good deal of the time either, but you will probably handle having too *little* to do better than you will handle having too *much* to do.

Score 16–25 points: You need a certain amount of stimulation and challenge in your job, and are restless when you have time on your hands; still, you are not one of those super people who thrive on pressure, and you're only capable of working under stress conditions for short periods of time. Finding the happy compromise between too much work and too little work is a real dilemma for you: you complain when you are overworked and you complain when you have nothing to do. Take some comfort from the fact that the majority of people in the world are very much like you; and it is for you and them that this chapter was written. Good luck finding your Ideal Job.

Score 26–30 points: Congratulations, you lucky superperson! Never, ever, will you have to be bored in a job since you are free to go after exhausting, demanding, exhilarating positions in which you have no *time* to be bored. You thrive on pressure, the more the better, and you won't get an ulcer or a heart attack from it either. You just love a desk piled up with projects, a cal-endar loaded up with appointments, a briefcase chock full of re-ports. And I bet you don't need more than five hours of sleep at night.

XX

The You Beneath the Title

OUR first important job comes to us like manna from the gods. After decades of struggling to achieve identity, after years of asking ourselves "Who am I?" and finding no meaningful answer beyond "son" or "daughter," "student," "husband" or "wife"—there it all is in a short, punchy phrase that defines us, explains us, justifies us.

John Doe, Marketing Director of Crumpton, Inc.
Jane Jones, Fashion Consultant for Flashiana Couture
Bob Smith, Subsidiary Rights Manager of Riffle Books
Ellen Strauss, Vice-President of Magnum Opus

An instant identity, and in capital letters, yet! What could be more delicious?

It's what everyone who *doesn't* have it is clamoring for. The restless housewives across the nation who are sick of being simply "Ed's wife" or "Jennifer's mother." The vast numbers of unemployed who, in addition to the more pressing and serious problem of poverty, are also, whether or not they even know it, seeking an identity to justify their lives. The elderly, forcibly retired, who once had it and have now lost it. That simple equation, "I = Job Title." It's the easiest way to carve an identify out of the conflicting, baffling, complex myriad of thoughts, perceptions, experiences, feelings, values, strengths, weaknesses, and impulses that constitute the "I."

And not only does it bring sense out of chaos for us, it brings instant recognition and respect from others.

I'm at a party among strangers, a party of important people. To introduce myself simply as "Addison Steele" leaves me feeling as naked as Adam felt right after he ate the apple. But oh what comfort, what confidence derives from being able to say, "I'm Addison Steele, Senior Editor at Keystone Press." No longer naked, I have invested myself in a tasteful, well-tailored identity. And in most cases the response is everything I could hope for: not the brush-off, "Nice to meet you," that would follow a mere, "Hello, I'm Addison Steele," but "Oh, *yes,* Mack Saunders at Prime Publishing has spoken of you often. Glad we finally have a chance to meet." It may not be the start of a profound lifetime friendship, but as cocktail party conversation goes, it's better than a kick in the teeth. And it gives me the inner security to walk up to the next stranger.

Yes, there's no doubt about it: Job identity is seductive, convenient, and ego-enhancing. All of the above. *Too much,* alas, of all of the above. It can also be poisonous.

We get used to it. We become increasingly dependent on it. And one day, soon, we wake up to find we can't get along without it. Then, if we lose it, God help us! We are devastated.

What we have done is to put all our ego-identity eggs in one basket—a basket owned by somebody else. This somebody, the corporation, has the power to take back the basket at any time, and our eggs right along with it.

So that if we lose our job—hardly a rare occurrence in corporate life—we are crushed by far more than worries over money, uncertainty about the future, or a feeling of failure. We add to this already heavy burden the additional trauma of our vanished identity. John Doe, Marketing Director of Crumpton, Inc., exists no longer. Who, then, is John Doe?

It comes down to this: The more one invests his ego in his professional identity, the more vulnerable he becomes to the vicissitudes of corporate life. People who would never in a million years willingly give anyone else power over where they live, what they eat, how they dress, or whom they see will thoughtlessly give others power over the most important single thing in their life—their identity.

But there is more to each and every one of us, thank heavens, than the particular position we hold at a particular time. And in order to cushion ourselves against possible future contingencies, it is absolutely essential that we learn to think in these terms.

Sometimes, as in the case of Brian, we can learn from the misfortunes of others.

"Two years ago," Brian told me, "a colleague of mine named Gene was fired from our office. He'd had a big job, Director of Sales, and he was making a high five-figure salary. So it wasn't easy for him to find another job at that kind of money, and he was out of work for a long time.

"He completely fell apart, went into a serious depression, and started to drink. And the thing is, it wasn't a question of money. Gene's in better financial shape than almost anyone I know; not only did he earn a lot of money when he was working, but he also inherited plenty from his father.

"It was the feeling of worthlessness that did it. Gene had eaten and slept that job for five years, to the point of ignoring everything else in his life. All his social activities—the golf club, the traveling, the nightlife—were built around his sales activities. All his friends were business contacts. When he lost his job, his golf foursome dropped him, the travel stopped, and he no longer "fit" into high-powered gatherings of business people. He had no hobbies, no outside interests to fall back on, and he became, quite literally, a man without an identity.

"I watched it happen," Brian continued, "and thought to myself that I wouldn't ever let that happen to me. That there was a lot more *to* me than my impressive-sounding position at ———.

"And a year later, during the height of the recession, I was let go. Everyone was very nice about it and said it was only because of 'the economic picture' or some such crap; and one of the Vice-Presidents asked me if I had any plans for the future. What plans could I possibly have had three hours after being told I was being terminated?

"At any rate, I told the V.P.—between clenched teeth, I imagine—that my major plan for the future was that I planned *not* to be devastated. I think those were my exact words: 'Being fired is reputed to be a devastating experience, and I plan not to be devastated.' I was thinking of Gene, of course. The Vice-President clapped me on the back and wished me luck, all the time thinking, I'm quite sure, what an *odd* thing to say.

"I decided it was high time I began thinking about who Brian Neely was, other than ex-Publicity Director at ————. That didn't mean I wasn't going to look for another job right away. But I knew the first thing, the most important thing, I had to do was something that would make me feel good about myself— something that *I*, and not anybody else, would be in control of. After all, trying to get another job puts you at the mercy of other people.

"I thought back to my college days when I was a pretty good amateur photographer and shot most of the pictures for the yearbook. I fished out my camera and started shooting scenes of the city, with an eye toward getting something accepted professionally. I put myself on a serious, disciplined schedule, so many hours a day, weather permitting. I even sold one shot of an old woman feeding a squirrel in Central Park, to a small journal you've probably never heard of.

"Then my wife, who was doing volunteer work for a local candidate running for election, suggested that with my publicity background I might be useful to the campaign, writing press releases and so forth. I volunteered and found that they were delighted to have me, although they couldn't pay me anything, of course. But I got to meet some interesting and important political people who valued me, my background, and my contribution. And it was fun—hectic, nonlucrative, but fun."

"How did all this extracurricular activity affect your job-hunting?" I asked.

"Well, the job-hunting had to take precedence, of course," Brian replied. "But the interesting part of it is the 'extracurricular activity,' as you call it, *helped* me get another job more quickly than I might have otherwise. If I'd gone on interviews feeling low and depressed and insignificant, I would have come across to potential employers as, well, *desperate*. Business people can smell that a mile off, as I'm sure you know. This way, I was confident and almost buoyant and made a much better impression. People are more likely to react favorably to you when you like yourself.

"So now I have an impressive new job identity, and I can't say I don't like it. But I'm still doing some photography on the weekends, and I hope maybe to sell another picture or two."

We can all profit from Brian's approach. Submerged, almost forgotten, beneath our professional niches in life is a versatile, multitalented human being with an identity that preceded, and will endure, after a particular job is lost. In fact, job specialization narrows us considerably, causing us to ignore a much wider spectrum of our individuality.

So, enjoy all the ego enhancement of a nifty professional identity. Why not?—you've earned it. But don't ever become too dependent on that identity: don't ever lose sight of the you that lurks beneath the title.

XXI

To Socialize or Not to Socialize?

SOME people go to the office, work more or less amicably with their business associates during the day, and go home in the evening to a full life totally outside their jobs.

Some people have an entire social life built around their work and their colleagues. They drink with them and dine with them, and sometimes even sleep with them, although the latter is not what we're discussing here.

Socializing with one's professional colleagues can be one of the most delightful aspects of a job. Anyone who has ever done so knows this is true. The liquor flows, the conversation is spirited, the feeling of comradeship is palpable, and the wit would grace the Algonquin Round Table. Away from the daily office grind in a social, relaxed setting, great good spirits are unleashed by great, common purpose.

People engaged in the same enterprise usually have a lot more to say to each other than people with disparate lives. Put together six or eight people at a suburban dinner party and the conversation may disintegrate to the lowest common denominator: the weather, rising taxes, and crabgrass. Put together six or eight people from the same office and you have all of them talking at once, gesturing wildly, interrupting, arguing, laughing. The conversation, the gossip, the outrageous anecdotes are interesting to each and every one of them because they've been there. They know the territory and they know all the principals.

In a nonbusiness group setting, you can tell me the funniest story about Jack and Joan at your office or Chester, your ex-college roommate, but if I don't know Jack or Joan or Chester, my interest will be marginal, no matter how entertaining the story.

But tell me a marginally interesting story about Maureen, the switchboard operator who's been listening in on all of our conversations for the past ten years, and I'm all ears, an ideal audience. Even if the story is only marginally interesting.

This is what makes afterwork socializing so seductive. All of our conversation is profoundly interesting—to us. An outsider among us would be bored to tears. But there are no outsiders among us. We are all great, good friends—for tonight, at any rate. And come tomorrow, everyone just *knows* we will bring that great good fellowship back to the office, back to the daily grind.

Or will we?

Seductive as after-hours socializing may be, there are pitfalls. And let me say at the outset that no one has enjoyed these high-spirited sessions more than I have. I have grooved—often—on the camaraderie, the humor, the intriguing gossip, the manic flow of conversation. Many of these get-togethers are occasions I still savor—occasions when Dottie Parker and Bob Benchley and George Kaufman had nothing on *us.*

But, alas, the pitfalls. I suppose you could call them the three Ps: *Politics, Pretense,* and *Pettiness.*

Politics: Is there one or more person in the group who is using this opportunity either to build himself up or tear others down?

Pretense: Are you free really to be yourself and say whatever comes into your mind, or are you on display, ever-mindful of the professional impression you are making?

Pettiness: Is there any viciousness to these evenings? Are there cliques forming? If you missed a session, would you be worried that people were talking unfavorably about *you?*

What it comes down to is that socializing after hours can't be divorced completely from office realities. Should you choose to indulge in it, you'd better have a pretty good idea as to the motivations of your colleagues. *You* may be going out for fun and relaxation. Other people may not be. And under the influence of liquor, good food, soft lights, and music, you will probably be careless. I should hope you *would* be careless! In fact, my argument is, *if you can't afford to be careless, can't afford to relax and say what you feel, then you shouldn't be out socializing in the first place.*

Under no circumstances should after-hours socializing be an ordeal where either your image or your future is on the line. If you have to walk on eggs, if you know you can't be too careful, then you need this added burden to an already long day like poison. Go home, take off your shoes, have a drink, curl up with your spouse, go to the movies, or have dinner with a childhood friend—*but don't subject yourself to corporate games carried beyond five o'clock,* at least not voluntarily. Let others expose their flanks, psyches, and other vulnerable parts. You stay clear.

Of course, there are such things as "command performances." The President of your company is having a birthday party at his Long Island estate, and you are invited. Your division is giving a dinner party for outside suppliers and you are one of the hosts. Fine. This isn't "socializing," this is business, pure and simple, and you are prepared. You will go, you will be charming, but you will also be "corporate." You will behave exactly as you would at a 10:00 A.M. marketing conference. You will be buttoned down and, even more important, buttoned up. You will not be remotely tempted to confuse business and pleasure. You, and everyone else, will be on guard.

But voluntary socializing should be loose, unpressured, and, above all, *safe.* If you get a little drunk, voice an uncorporate sentiment or two, you should be able to go home and sleep comfortably, knowing no real harm has been done.

Chuck, the magazine staff writer I interviewed in an earlier chapter, was obliged to watch his afterwork socializing go from the sublime to the ridiculous. And eventually he was forced to give it up entirely.

"Roy, my first boss, was the guiding spirit behind many of our evening get-togethers, and during the five years he ran the Editorial Department these sessions became sort of a tradition," Chuck told me. "Roy had come up through the ranks and everyone was comfortable with him. In the office he was the boss, but after hours all of us sort of forgot about his position. Roy forgot about it, too. He loved to drink, loved to throw the bull, and wanted to get away completely from questions of rank, seniority, and power. We would bitch good-naturedly about the organization right in front of him as though he were just another colleague, and sometimes, usually after a second or third drink, he'd bitch right along with us. A few of these evenings lasted until one or two in the morning. We all felt we would die for one another, and the morale was terrific.

"Roy left and Geller took over. Somehow he heard about our midweek gatherings and he conspired to come along whenever we got together.

"Well, first of all, no one was comfortable with Geller—at best, he was an unknown quantity—and the sessions became extremely stiff. People stopped saying whatever came into their minds and began trying to impress Geller. But that's bound to happen at first with a new man, and I thought it would stop after a while. However, Geller encouraged it. He considered after-five socializing to be merely an extension of the business day and availed himself of every opportunity to learn more about his staff.

"I began to hear stories that made me extremely uneasy. It seemed that Geller would encourage people to say some pretty impolitic things at these sessions while remaining noncommittal himself. Then a couple of people told me he had flung their ill-considered remarks back in their faces during key moments at the office. One guy claimed it cost him a raise, and another guy said his expense account was slashed twenty percent as a result."

"The socializing must have stopped pretty quickly," I hazarded.

Chuck shook his head emphatically.

"You'd be surprised," he said, "but it didn't stop at all. It just changed. People knew Geller was using these sessions to get the lowdown on them, so they began using the opportunity to try and impress him. Two hours of drinking in a downstairs bar became indistinguishable from a two-hour meeting in the conference room. It was tense as hell."

"Why did the staff continue to go out with him?" I asked.

Chuck thought about that for a minute.

"Well, fear, for one thing," he said. "Everyone was afraid they'd be conspicuous by their absence if they suddenly stopped going along, and that Geller would bear a grudge. And maybe they were afraid people would talk about them behind their backs if they weren't there to protect themselves.

"Ambition second. They thought they could use the out-of-office opportunity to get an inside track with Geller and get a leg up over the opposition. And they knew if they didn't, someone else would. They thought they couldn't afford to bypass that chance.

"And, I suspect, arrogance had a little to do with it, too. No one wanted to admit that he couldn't drink and stay on his guard at the same time. Although the amount of liquor consumed went down drastically, I'll tell you that."

"What made *you* stop going?" I asked.

"I saw no reason to add three or four unnecessary, tension-filled hours to an already long, tension-filled day," Chuck replied. "This was my free time, something I have little enough of, God knows! I wasn't going to waste it on that sort of unpleasantness. Besides, by that time I didn't really care about the job. I hated Geller, hated his deviousness and what he'd done to department morale, and I was looking for another job. So it was a matter of complete indifference to me what he thought. Anyway, what could he do? What could he have done to anyone? You could always say that you had plans that night, or that you'd been neglecting your children and your wife was threatening you with divorce. No one has to put up indefinitely with that sort of thing."

Chuck's right. No one does. And no one *should* have to. Social occasions should be exactly that—social. They are most certainly not the time for politics and one-upmanship and worry.

Nor are they an occasion for the cementing of office cliques, a poisonous enough situation when it occurs during office hours (and one that you would be well advised to stay out of at all costs), but absolutely to be avoided after hours. This is the "pettiness" we were referring to earlier, in its own way just as potentially destructive as politics. The existence of cliques within an office is almost always a symptom of more fundamental maladies: competition, distrust, jealousy, and job insecurity. *Don't play along.* Maintain amicable relations with everyone in the office as far as possible, and turn a deaf ear and a blind eye to any personal pettiness you happen to see around you. Never bad-mouth one co-worker to another: It will get back; it always does. And it will give others a pretty decent excuse to badmouth *you*.

Perhaps you are worried that if you don't go along for these after-hours sessions, cliquish or not, other people are going to gossip about you. Perhaps, but if they are into petty gossip, they are going to gossip about you whether or not you go along. (They'll find an occasion when you're not there, don't worry.) By not going along, by not involving yourself with cliques, you are eliminating much of what they will be able to find to *say* about you. And if they don't have much to say about you, they'll soon move on to somebody else.

In conclusion: After-hours socializing is supposed to *decrease* tension, not *increase* it. Never forget the purpose of socializing, which is enjoyment. If and when it stops being fun, drop out and find something more pleasurable to do with your free time. Like Chuck, you have little enough of it!

XXII

How Much Is Your Time Worth?

TIME is money, goes the old cliché, but it's really much more important than that. Sell your time for money alone and you've made a bad bargain, *no matter how high the purchase price.* What's the point of making a hundred grand a year if you only have four and a half hours a week to enjoy it?

What about your family, you might ask? They will surely have time to enjoy it.

That's true, of course. But if you think that way, you are a nobler, more altruistic person than I am. I, for one, want plenty of leisure time to enjoy the fruits of my own labor.

So I would define an ideal working life as one in which excess salary is used to purchase excess time. In fact, I have derived a formula:

Steele's Formula No. 1

$$Mt = mT \text{ (where } M > m)$$

In this equation, M represents the amount of money you earn in twelve months; m stands for the amount of money you need to live comfortably, according to your own needs, extravagances, and responsibilities. T is equal to a twelve-month working year (if you work only a nine-month year, then T = 9). And t is a shorter working year than you are now working. We then solve the equation for t, to be expressed in number of months worked in a year.

Let's say you found when you were making twenty thousand dollars a year that you were able to live pretty much as you wanted to. Now it's three years later and, while your expenses have not increased too drastically, your salary has shot up to thirty thousand. But you don't have nearly as much time to enjoy it as you used to; you are working longer and longer hours.

At this stage of your life, time is more precious to you than money. (This state of affairs can change at any moment, of course.) But wouldn't it be wonderful if right now you could purchase additional free time with the extra money?

According to the formula:

$$Mt = mT$$
$$30,000 \times t = 20,000 \times 12$$
$$t = 8$$

You can work an eight-month year and make enough money to live according to your present needs.

Leaving aside for a moment the question of whether your company would allow you to buy back four months a year (they probably wouldn't, but we're talking about ideal formulas, not existing realities), this equation rests on several underlying assumptions:

1. $M > m$: that is, you are making more money than you feel you need, a situation which, admittedly, not many people are fortunate enough to be in.
2. You enjoy your free time more than your on-the-job time, which is certainly not true of everybody. (The people who prefer work to leisure will be discussed later in this chapter.)
3. That if you had more leisure time, you would not spend more money than you are spending now, for if you did, that would change the m of the equation.

But, you might ask, if companies are going to continue to demand full-time work from their employees regardless of their re-

spective financial situations, then why have I bothered to include this time-money equation in the first place? It's completely impractical and not worth thinking about for that reason.

It may, perhaps, be impractical, but I feel it is very much
worth thinking about as a tool for putting the proper *value* on
your time. It makes clear that time is something *worth* spending
money for—at least as much so as a bigger house or a second
car. Moreover, it demonstrates that once your house is a nice,
big house, and you are thinking about a third car, maybe the
circumstances are now such that time is the most valuable commodity you can buy. Certainly if I had used as my example not a
person going from twenty to thirty thousand dollars a year, but a
person going from seventy-five to a *hundred* thousand dollars a
year, the point would have been made much more strongly. At
some salary level, the need for money must become less great
than the need for leisure time, and any further sacrifice of that
time then becomes self-defeating.

Unless, of course, you would rather work than do anything
else. There are lots of people who would; and a large majority of
them, with very good reason, are extremely successful.

You may recall that, at the outset of this chapter, I said that if
you sell your time for money alone, you have made a bad bargain. The key word here is "alone." If from those long hours you
are getting excitement, stimulation, variety, and fulfillment in
greater quantity than you ever derive from your leisure activities, then you have made a very good bargain. And if, in addition,
you are extremely well paid, then you have made an even better
bargain.

There exists, after all, a type of person who has come to be
known as a "workaholic." It is, I believe, an unfortunate term,
for as much as I may be unable to fathom such a personality, I
respect the inclinations and temperament of the individuals
who fall into this category. (Some of them are neurotic and
compensating for emotional lacks in their lives, sure—but there
are plenty of neurotics among the hedonistic, too.) Many work-
aholics are simply outstanding, dynamic, energetic, and happy
people with extremely full lives. It's just that they've never

found any leisure pursuit to compete with the excitement they derive from their work. Speak to them in terms of "selling their time" to the corporation and they will stare at you blankly. Money is not the point, it just isn't.

They do, however, say and do some of the *damnedest* things! Bob, an Editorial General Manager, told me some marvelous anecdotes about Laura, the Vice-President of his division, and a dyed-in-the-wool workaholic.

"She's known for it," he said, "not only in our company, but throughout the business. Even if I hadn't already known how she felt about work, I would have been tipped off by the statement she made to me upon returning from a two-week vacation in the Caribbean.

" 'I just *love* vacations,' she burbled unself-consciously. 'You can get so much work done.'

"That," Bob continued, "set the stage for the morning Laura was late arriving at work. Late for Laura, you have to realize, was nine-fifteen. But since she was almost always in the office by eight in the morning, by nine-fifteen everyone was picturing her dead in the gutter, lying in a pool of blood. I sound as though I'm kidding, but actually I'm not. We really *were* worried.

"The mystery was explained once Laura arrived. It seems she had stayed late at the office the night before. OK, so she stayed late; she often does. *But Laura had not left the office until seven-thirty in the morning.* She had gone home briefly for a shower and breakfast. And she was back by nine-fifteen, mumbling apologies about being late. No one could believe it, but Laura didn't seem to see anything especially unusual about it. She did make one concession, however—she went home that night at six-thirty."

I was silent for a moment, not sure whether to count Laura a superwoman or a fool.

"What's she like?" I asked Bob.

He laughed.

"Forget it, you won't win this one. She's thirty-six years old. She's attractive and well adjusted. She's married to an attractive, well-adjusted, successful man and has two attractive, well-adjusted children. She is also—although I shouldn't really tell you this—having an affair with a famous author you've probably heard of. And I hope you're not going to ask me where she finds the time, because I haven't the slightest idea."

"The rich are different from you and me," I said, awed. "So, too, are the energetic."

"You'd better believe it," Bob responded.

Let's move on now from Laura to someone who is not quite so extraordinary.

Craig, a bachelor, is one of the few people who did not shake his head in disbelief when I showed him the Mt = mT formula. As a bachelor, he is not under financial pressure to earn ever-increasing sums of money. Moreover, Craig is one of those people who prefers his leisure activities to his working life: Surely, he maintains, it ought to be obvious to any sane individual that riding a horse along the beach or landing a trout in a mountain stream is a lot more fun than working in an office. Craig is a sports fanatic who rides, hunts, sails, fishes, and plays tennis. If he had been less bright and well-educated, he might have run off to tend cattle in Argentina instead of becoming a middle manager working with his brains instead of his hands. Leisure time for Craig is far more precious than any material possession: He lives in a rundown rent-controlled apartment that, possibly, no eyes but his have ever seen, but he takes fabulous, exotic vacations into the uncharted wilderness of Central and South America.

He therefore agreed instantly with the philosophy behind my formula.

"Mt = mT?" he mused. "That's pretty good. I've never heard it expressed that way before. Where did you pick it up?"

"I created it myself," I replied grandly. "My very own formula."

"It *has* something," Craig said with a smile. "Perhaps a bit less than E = mc², but, as homemade equations go, it's not half bad.

"Besides," he continued, "it's an idea. I'm tempted to put

into practice. How do you think the President of the company would respond if I told him I could afford to work an eight-month year?"

"I suspect you shouldn't try to find out," I said.

Craig sighed.

"No, I don't suppose I should. But it's a provocative idea all the same."

"Do you think you and I are atypical in the value we give to free time?" I asked.

"No, I don't," he answered. "Definitely not. You would be amazed how many highly successful people I know—not only businessmen but professionals as well—who have admitted in weak moments that their work is not nearly as challenging and stimulating as it sounds on paper, and that they could give up much of it or even all of it in a minute. The people who have admitted that aren't, however, people I work with; the people I work with would be afraid to admit to a colleague that they are anything less than totally devoted to their jobs and to the firm. They're afraid that any sentiment to the contrary would jeopardize their positions and their futures. But I'm sure I'm far from the only person there who is often bored and restless and would like more time to do other things."

IF Craig's (and my) philosophy seems subversive in light of the deep-rooted Puritan Ethic and Horatio Alger myth, I would protest that the advertising community in the United States doesn't appear to think so. Said community always has—or tries to have—its finger on the pulse of America. And lately I have noticed—and I suspect you *also* have noticed—a distinct bias in the direction of leisure time. To wit:

"Weekends are made for Michelob."

And, to wit again:

"We're AMF. We make weekends."

To whom is the advertising community speaking? Are they speaking only to bored assembly-line workers in the automobile industry? Are they speaking only to frustrated drudges in the typing pool?

I think not. Because the advertising community always, by its very nature, tries to reach as large a consumer audience as possible, I think they are speaking to *all* of us, however exalted our professional rank may be. They are saying: "We don't care *how* glamorous your job may look to the outside; we know (and possibly they have done research to show) that you value your leisure enormously, whatever you might or might not say for the benefit of other people. We are advertising your dreams—your dreams of stepping off the treadmill, if only for forty-eight hours at a time."

Perhaps you do not fit into this category. Perhaps forty-eight hours a week is as much leisure time as you want or you need. But take my word for it: A lot of bright, educated, talented people would dearly love to have more. And it is for them that the Mt = mT formula was devised.

XXIII
Are Office Friendships Hazardous to Your Career?

THERE is a prevailing philosophy in the corporate world, even among individuals who are decent and not excessively ambitious, that close friendships in an office are risky to establish and impossible to maintain. Although I, personally, refuse to share in such cynicism, I am going to start off this chapter with a rather cynical story.

It's the story of a friend who had a friend, or *thought* she had a friend, in the office. I'll call my friend Brenda, and I'll call Brenda's friend Joan.

Brenda and Joan had much in common besides their jobs on the staff of a major women's magazine. Both were divorced and struggling to bring up two pre-teenage children. Both were active in feminist organizations. And both were originally from the Midwest. They were a great deal closer than are most office acquaintances. And they were more candid with each other than most office acquaintances: They discussed freely their mutual loathing for their new boss, a notably power-hungry, ruthless female executive.

Probably, Brenda admitted to me, she had been less successful in hiding her loathing from her boss than had Joan. At any rate, Brenda was fired. Because of her heavy family responsibilities, the termination was an unmitigated personal disaster, and the only solace on that black day was the way her colleagues flocked to her side. Even people she had not been particularly close to said all the right things: "You know this had nothing to do with your professional performance—you're one of the most valuable people here—it's simply a personality clash. You'll get a terrific job very soon, I'm sure of it." Others said things like: "You are so lucky to be out of this awful situation. In a way I envy you. Your next job simply *has* to be more pleasant."

And what did her good friend, her bosom friend, Joan, say? What she said was:

"Brenda, did you get any sort of warning before she fired you?"

"My God," Brenda told me, "I knew then that all Joan was thinking about was her own skin. I was terribly hurt, and for a couple of weeks I had no desire ever to speak to her again. Then I thought, I'm being childish. People don't always say the perfect thing in awkward situations. Besides, Joan's friendship was important to me. I didn't want to give it up.

"So I called her, and we set up a date. She was going to come over to my house at six o'clock one evening.

"She wasn't there at six. She wasn't there at six-thirty. She wasn't there at six forty-five. At seven o'clock I called her house. When she got on the phone I realized, straight off, that she had forgotten all about it, although she tried to cover it up by saying she had gone home sick and fallen asleep. I played along with her, although perhaps I shouldn't have, and then she blew it. She said—and you're not going to believe this—she said, 'That will teach me not to write things down in code.'

"I was stunned. Not because I didn't know what she was talking about, but because I instantly knew *exactly* what she was talking about. And I blurted out, 'You mean you're afraid that Phyllis'—that's the boss—'will find out you had drinks with me tonight?'

" 'I don't want any trouble,' Joan said to me, and that really tore it for me. Even so, I did not give vent to my anger; rather, I tried to reason with her. I said to her, in as even a tone of voice as I could manage, 'Joan, for heaven's sake, this awful woman dominates every minute of your working day. She would dearly love to dominate every minute of your *non*working day as well. *Are you going to let her?* Are you going to allow her to dictate whom you may and may not see after hours? If so, you're giving her more power over your life than even the organization permits.

"Joan then repeated to me, 'Brenda, I'm not looking for trouble. I simply can't afford it right now.'

"And thus ended the phone call. And thus, too, ended our friendship. R.I.P."

An appalling story, yes? Fortunately this is an extreme case in which the instinct for self-preservation at the expense of personal relationships is carried to a degree well beyond the norm.

But less extreme examples abound. Many people in the business world unemotionally accept the premise that personal friendships must realistically take a back seat to corporate survival and/or advancement.

Why is it that such friendships are viewed by so many career-minded people as strictly *verboten*? What are they afraid of?

They are afraid of what I choose to call the "what ifs" of office relationships:

1. What if a current friend and co-worker becomes a subordinate in the future and you have to deal with him in a boss/underling framework?

2. What if you and your friend find yourself in competition for the same promotion?

3. What if your friend and you one day find yourselves on different rungs of the corporate ladder?

4. What if you confide your secret weaknesses, job irritations, and reservations about the company to a friend? Are you leaving yourself vulnerable to being stabbed in the back?

5. And what if you *don't* confide any of the above to your friend because the risk is too great? Is there such a thing as a close friendship when the people involved can never really level with each other about the things that matter?

These are all legitimate concerns, but none, I maintain, justifies the abandoning of a friendship which is really important to you.

As usual, it is the overtly ambitious who suffer least from the dilemma. They choose, often quite consciously, simply never to *have* friends at the office. And not all of them are cold and remote, either. Many are what I would call "good back-slappers." An occasional free-wheeling lunch (*you* free-wheel, *they* listen); some irreverent stabs at the Personnel Department (*you* stab, *they* chuckle); once in a while a strong shoulder for you to lean on (they may need your loyalty at some point in the future)—this is the nature of the "friendship." Nothing that would ever prove inconvenient. Nothing that would ever hold them back from future corporate advancement. They have made their choice—and for them (here is the rub), it isn't even painful. Success *über alles*.

But for so many of us, putting advancement ahead of relationships *is* a painful choice. And, if it is not in your nature to do so, any such sacrifice of your own interests and integrity will produce at best a bad taste in the mouth, at worst a profound feeling of self-loathing.

Let's deal one by one with the "what ifs" of office friendships. Let's examine if the pitfalls are dire enough to justify living your corporate life in splendid emotional isolation and distrust.

1. What if your current friend and co-worker becomes a subordinate in the future?

This is potentially the thorniest of all possible developments. But remember: no genuine friend who is sensitive to your problems and needs will deliberately take advantage of that relationship, especially if it means putting you in an impossible situation. You should assume that he will bend over backward to avoid putting you on the spot; moreover, you should assume he is bright enough to realize that any attempt on his part to take advantage of your liking for him may put an abrupt end to your friendship.

Supposing you find yourself in a situation where you have to criticize either his work or his behavior? This is tricky. But one executive went so far as to tell me that criticizing a friend can actually be easier than criticizing someone with whom you have little rapport. There is an underlying atmosphere of good will that takes the personal sting out of the criticism and makes clear you are speaking on a purely professional, objective level. And because the subordinate likes you so much, he will be unusually anxious to please you. He will also be rooting for your corporate success, a statement which can hardly be made about all subordinates.

Of course, you will not be able to confide your management problems to a friend whom you supervise. This will make the relationship less open and spontaneous and will probably produce some strain—perhaps too much for the friendship to withstand, perhaps not. It will depend on how important a part candid conversation about the office once played in your relationship. If the strain becomes too great, the problem will take care of itself: the friendship will self-destruct. But don't *you* be the one to cast aside your friend four hours after your exciting new promotion. If the relationship will no longer work, then so be it—but let it die of its own accord. Don't assassinate it.

2. What if you and your friend find yourself in competition for the same promotion?

My reply to that is: so what? If you're going to lose out, you're going to lose out. Wouldn't you rather see the plum go to a cherished friend than to a hated enemy? You can be honest with your friend; honesty is the basis of all good relationships. All you have to say is: "You know, Jim, I really want to head that department, and I think I'd be good at it. But if I don't get the job, I hope you do."

3. What if your friend and you one day find yourselves on different rungs of the corporate ladder?

Answer: It will be good for both your souls. The snobbery that exists in corporations over rank in the hierarchy is absolutely mind-boggling. Is your position so tenuous, so fragile, so vulnerable to every breeze of gossip that filters through the office that it can be threatened by—gasp—a friendship with someone who has a lowlier title, a smaller office, and less clout than you?

We're back to appearances. People worry over what other people will think. People have been known to give up friendships because of what other people may think. Frankly, my dear, I don't think you should give a damn.

4. What if you confide your secret weaknesses, job irritations, and reservations about the company to a friend? Are you leaving yourself vulnerable to being stabbed in the back?

It's risky—very risky—and you had better be awfully sure your confidant is really a trusted friend. One way of being sure is to notice how open and self-revealing he is to you. Risky confidences should never be a one-way street: if the friendship is genuine, you will both trust each other enough to speak your minds without fear that what you are saying will get back to anyone else. And if the trust is there, if you can count on even one person in the office who really cares about you, what a terrific and tension-reducing outlet for your most burdensome job worries. After all, you can tell a friend or lover outside the office some of the things that are upsetting or disturbing to you and they will offer a safe and genuinely concerned shoulder. But because they are not intimately involved with the people and the situation, they may not be able to offer much in the way of help. A good office friend, however, will most certainly be more helpful, and, because he or she knows the lay of the land, may be a lot more soul-satisfying to talk to. It's an outlet that can save ulcers, believe me.

5. What if you *don't* confide in your friend? Is there such a thing as a close friendship when the people involved can never really level with each other about the things that matter?

Close, no. When so many feelings, concerns, and anxieties are tacitly defined as "off-limits" by both parties, the relationship can never be much more than pleasantly superficial. But the pleasantly superficial is hardly to be despised. Profound relationships, both in and outside the office, are extremely rare. We all round them out with enjoyable, if not enormously intense, relationships; if we didn't, our circle of friends would be small indeed. There is a place at the office for the superficial friend whom you wouldn't necessarily confide in, as well as a place for the completely trusted friend who may be saving you from ulcers. As long as you don't confuse the one with the other, you can have the best of both worlds.

To sum up: You spend an enormous chunk of your life in the office. If you deny yourself the pleasure and comfort of having good friends there for reasons of ambition and/or fear, you have cut yourself off from a most fulfilling and important aspect of human existence. And life is much too short for that.

XXIV
Keeping a Sense of Perspective

Do you remember that well-worn joke about the man who brags to his friend: "I make the major decisions; my wife makes the minor decisions. She decides where we should live, how we should spend our money, where the kids should go to school. I decide whether Communist China should be admitted to the UN."?

Probably. And perhaps you are also familiar with the old newspaper adage about what sort of tragedy best sells newspapers: "A *million* deaths five thousand miles away equals a *hundred* deaths five hundred miles away equals *one* death next door."

We are all—bless our souls—extremely solipsistic creatures. Nothing wrong with that, except when it makes us absolutely miserable. And in our corporate life it makes us absolutely miserable as often as not.

A single criticism by a boss, one ominously worded office memo, a lone business deal we failed to close, and we can brood for weeks. Meanwhile, we may learn that seventeen potentially belligerent nations have developed an atomic weapon; that our city is about to go into bankruptcy; that the world's climate is undergoing a possibly disastrous transformation, and we won't worry about it for more than eleven seconds—or at least not until it touches *us*..

On the brighter side, we may fail to notice how radiantly the sun is shining, how beautiful the leaves are, and how sweet the flowers smell. Last *month* we may have noticed—before that ominously worded memo appeared on our desk—but right now all the wonders of the world are blocked out in an overwhelming fit of office panic. And anyway, when was the last time we had a free moment to smell the flowers?

We have lost our sense of proportion. Caught up in the minutiae of our daily grind, we forget there is a beautiful, intricate, awe-inspiring, uncertain, multifaceted world out there. It is a world that will continue in its complicated, untidy way whether or not Smith gets that corner office, Jones is selected to handle the major account, and Brown doesn't like the first paragraph of our marketing report. Or even the first *seven* paragraphs. Or, heaven forbid, the whole report.

The *big* problems in any job, quite obviously, can hardly be defined as minutiae. If there is a chance that you are going to be fired or painted into an unacceptable corner, the very real concern over supporting a family and paying the bills will, QED, take precedence over any worry about nuclear warfare, climate changes, or, on the brighter side, a sudden compulsion to smell the flowers. All of us have times in any job where there are major legitimate problems that could transform our lives, and with which we must seriously contend.

But so much of our concern, such an overwhelming proportion of it, is pure corporate trivia—the sort of Mickey Mouse jockeying for position that we have been discussing in previous chapters. What we need is a breath of fresh air, and I mean this literally: it would do most of us good to go and stand on a remote mountaintop far from our frenetic incorporated surroundings and take huge gulps of the pure, invigorating air. *I won't get that corner office.* Gulp. *Algernon Horatio is closer to the boss than I am.* Gulp. *I have to share a secretary with that conniving son-of-a-bitch, Joe Sammyrun.* Gulp, gulp.

So it's unfortunate. So whoever said life was perfect? Keep a sense of perspective. You can still put food on the table. You still have a roof over your head. They haven't fired you yet and probably won't. And there's an absolutely spectacular view stretching below you that predates by millions of years *your* corporation and *my* corporation and *all* corporations. There's a beautiful world that exists outside of interoffice memos, sales charts, trumped-up statistics, computer printouts, and bottom lines. And sometimes you have to get away from those pressures to remember it.

The vast number of hours we spend in the corporate world makes keeping a sense of perspective extremely difficult. Most employees have as little as two weeks and no more than four weeks off each year. That leaves between forty-eight and fifty weeks each year in which the corporate environment looms as the center of our universe. And the more we are committed to our jobs, the more we enjoy our work and want to do well at it, the more we suffer from corporate claustrophobia. The people who are merely going through the motions, the people who are simply collecting their paychecks—these are not the people I am addressing. They already *have* a sense of priorities: they believe work is a necessary evil and they don't expect to get fulfillment or excitement from it. Consequently, they are hardly likely to make *any* corporation the center of their existence. Consequently, they may already be standing on that mountaintop, even though they need those breaths of fresh air a lot less than we do.

But if we all could learn to keep a sense of perspective about our corporate lives, how much less vulnerable we would be to every passing irritation, disappointment, and manipulation that comes our way. If, instead of reaching for a martini or a tranquilizer, we could recharge our overworked batteries with a "fix" of something enduring—a mountain, the ocean, a great work of art, a symphonic masterpiece—we might better see where our beloved corporation stands in the great scheme of things. For, in the great scheme of things, our beloved corporation doesn't count for very much at all.

But people count. Essential decency counts. Friendship counts. Honesty counts. Liking oneself counts. And these things are too important to sacrifice for corporate advancement.

So do go to that metaphorical mountaintop from time to time, whenever you are suffering from corporate claustrophobia. There's a beautiful, unincorporated world out there. Try never to lose sight of it.

THE MAN FROM LISBON

Thomas Gifford

He swindled his way from the steaming rain forests of Angola to the wealth and glamour of 1920's Biarritz, Paris and London. They called him The Man From Lisbon but there was nothing anonymous about Alves Reis. In 1925 he perpetrated the most astounding confidence trick the world has ever known. It catapulted him to a position of enormous power, made him richer by $5,000,000, and brought down a government. His aim was financial control of Portugal. His methods were extraordinary. His story is unforgettable – and true.

* Also by Thomas Gifford and available from Futura – *The Wind Chill Factor*, *The Cavanaugh Quest*

UNQUIET SOUL

Margot Peters

'A totally fascinating book about the Brontës – perhaps the best ever published' *Irving Stone*

'The story itself is so gripping and the telling is so good that one ceases to question and reads on to weep . . . a most readable book that cannot fail to move' *Margaret Drabble*

'This fine biography is both moving and revealing . . . a compelling narrative, never marred with indiscriminate sympathising' *Spectator*

A CHILD IN THE FOREST

Winifred Foley

'A winner . . . a vivid and personal story of the life and hardships faced by a Forest of Dean miner's family in the 1920's . . . a moving commentary on the Forest way of life as seen through the eyes of a child'
Gloucestershire Life

'A land of oak and fern, of secret hill farms and plain, matter of fact market towns . . . Still a Forester, Winifred Foley recalls vividly but unsentimentally the loving, poverty-stricken home where she was brought up'
Birmingham Post

'Warm-hearted and well-observed' *Sunday Telegraph*

'The story is funny and touching by turns' *Manchester Evening News*

A CHILD IN THE FOREST is the book on which the Radio 4 Woman's Hour serial of the same name and the BBC 1 television film, ABIDE WITH ME, was based.

All Futura Books are available at your bookshop or newsagent, or can be ordered from the following address:
Futura Books, Cash Sales Department,
P.O. Box 11, Falmouth, Cornwall.

Please send cheque or postal order (no currency), and allow 25p for postage and packing for the first book plus 10p per copy for each additional book ordered up to a maximum charge of £1.05 in U.K.

Customers in Eire and B.F.P.O. please allow 25p for postage and packing for the first book plus 10p per copy for the next eight books, thereafter 5p per book.

Overseas customers please allow 40p for postage and packing for the first book and 12p per copy for each additional book.